Welcome to Würzburg!

"Würzburg is one of those cities that emits a feeling of delight upon hearing its name; it makes the heart beat a little faster." Like Josef Hofmiller, many a well known and many a lesser well known visitor has thoroughly enjoyed a visit to our city.

Its lovely location in the Main River valley and its numerous unique cultural monuments all contribute to the city's attractiveness and its reconstruction after the war has once again turned it into one of Germany's most charming and likeable cities. Würzburg, the city of art, culture and the sciences, is also the center of the Franconian winegrowing region.

This tourist guide offers a comprehensive overview not only of the city's history and sights, it is also choked full of useful information that will enable you to make the most of Würzburg's congenial ambiance and hospitality.

I wish you a most pleasant stay here and many a memorable moment.

Georg Rosenthal
Lord Mayor

Welcome to the Main-Franconian Metropolis

WÜRZBURG
City Guide

Photography: Elmar Hahn
Text: Christine Weisner
Concept: Klaus Schinagl
English: Dr. Terence Zuber

Würzburg at a Glance

including more than 120 color photos, a city map, orientation
plan, practical information, cultural events and local festivals

elmar
hahn
verlag

ISBN 978-3-928645-61-4

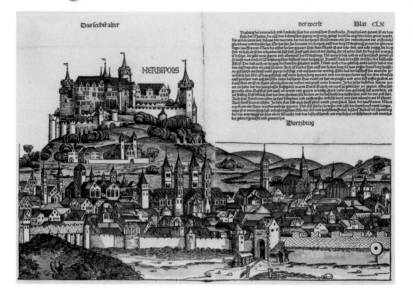

Milestones in Würzburg's History

Sometime after 1000 BCE First fortification on the Marienberg

Circa 500 BCE Celtic princely residence on the Marienberg Hill

100 BCE Germanic tribes (Burgundians, Alemanni and Thuringians) move into the region

Circa 500 CE Expansion of the Franks along the Main River

Circa 600 Seat of the Main-Franconian dukes, the fortification of the Marienberg around the Burkard quarter and a duke's court on the right side of the river

689 Martyrdom of the Irish missionaries: Kilian, Kolonat and Totnan

704 First official record of "castellum Virteburch"

706 Consecration of the first church on the Marienberg

742 Boniface founds the bishopric; Burkard serves as the first bishop

788 Consecration of the first Cathedral in the presence of Charlemagne

Before 1000 Fortification of the settlement around the Bishop's Miter

1133 First stone bridge across the Main River is erected

1147 First pogrom against the Jewish population; further pogroms follow in 1188 and 1298

1156 Emperor Frederick Barbarossa marries Beatrice of Burgundy in Würzburg

1168 Frederick Barbarossa confers the ducal title on the bishop in Würzburg

Circa 1200 Expansion of the city walls; the population is around 5,000

1201 Bishop Konrad von Querfurt has the Marienberg Fortress built as his residence

Circa 1230 Walther von der Vogelweide is buried in the Lusam Garden of the Neumünster Church

1316 City purchases the Grafeneckart building to be used as its town hall

1316/19 Bürgerspital Charitable Institution is founded

1349	Pogrom on the Market Place drives out the remaining Jews
1377	Foundation stone to Mary's Chapel laid where the former synagogue stood
1400	Bishop's troops defeat the burghers at the Battle of Bergtheim
1402	Founding of the first university
1518	Martin Luther pays two visits to the city
1525	Townspeople and peasants are defeated during the Peasants' War
1576	Julius Echter founds the Juliusspital Charitable Institution and
1582	a new university
1631	Swedes lay siege to the town and the fortress
As of 1650	Johann Philipp von Schönborn has Baroque fortifications built
1720	Construction of the Residence under Philipp Franz von Schönborn begins
1749	One of the last witch trials ends with the execution of the nun, Maria Renata Singer
1753	Completion of Tiepolo's frescos in the Residence
1796	French Revolutionary Army lays siege to the town; French troops depart after their defeat by Archduke Charles of Austria in a battle near Würzburg
1802/03	Würzburg is annexed to Bavaria; the first Protestants and Jews return to the city
1804	First theater is built
1806	Würzburg becomes a Grand Duchy under Ferdinand of Tuscany
1814	Final integration into Bavaria
1817	Koenig & Bauer High Speed Printing Machine Company opens its factory in the secularized convent in Oberzell
1841	Beginning of large-scale commercial shipping on the river
1852	Würzburg has around 30,000 inhabitants

1854	City is linked to the German rail system
1866	Prussians bombard the fortress during the Austro-Prussian War
As of 1868	Würzburg begins tearing down its fortified walls and turns the area into a Ring Park; new streets are laid out
1892	First horse-drawn streetcar in the city
1895	Wilhelm Conrad Röntgen discovers the x-ray in Würzburg
1905	Population reaches 80,000
1922	First Mozart Festival is held
1930	Community of Heidingsfeld is incorporated into the city
May 3, 1933	National Socialist Party receives 31.46% of the vote in Würzburg
June 17, 1943	Last Jews in the city are deported
March 16, 1945	British Air Force bombs the city and approximately 5,000 people lose their lives; the Old Town lies in rubble
1947	Main-Franconian Museum opens its doors at the Marienberg
1962	Caen and Dundee become sister cities; over time Würzburg is a sister city to Rochester, Mwana, Otsu, Salamanca, Suhl, Umea and Bray
1964	City is connected to the autobahn
1965	Construction begins on the university campus on Hubland hill
1973	Würzburg is conferred the title of a "European City"
1974/78	Outlying communities are incorporated and the city establishes its current size
2002	Kulturspeicher or Granary Museum opens its doors
2004	City celebrates its 1300th anniversary
2007	Museum Shalom Europa opens its doors

Above: The oldest view of Würzburg from Schedel's "Chronicle of the World"; woodcarving 1493.

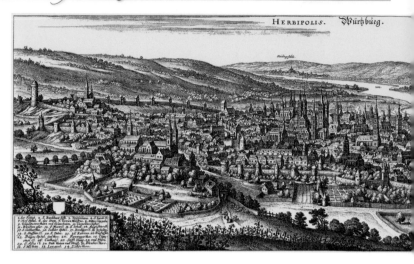

HERBIPOLIS. Würtzburg.

The Church, Wine and Science

The bishops ruled Würzburg and its **bishopric** for over a thousand years. The numerous spires and steeples that still dominate the skyline pay tribute to their sovereignty as does the **Residence**, the palace that Napoleon once called the most beautiful parsonage in Europe.

The power of the bishops ended around two hundred years ago. The former Baroque city did not transform itself into an important industrial center in the 19th century. Instead, the city decided that other factors such as the university, the quality of life, and its charming location on the Main River as well as the surrounding vineyard slopes needed to be emphasized. And fortunately, these factors still apply.

The Favorable Location

The mild climate in the valley along with the river and the relatively steep slopes of the fortress hill were reason enough for early settlement in the area. The oldest traces date back to 5600 BCE. As of around 1000 BCE, **Marienberg hill** was forti-

fied for the first time. Powerful Celtic tribal princes already lived here in the pre-Christian Hallstattian era and could afford luxury items such as the shards of Greek ceramic excavated here bear witness to. Around 100 BCE Burgundians, Alemanni and Thuringians began to settle in the region and around 500 CE the Franks migrated as far as the Main River region and began exerting their influence.

A Thriving Common Goal

Over 1300 years ago in 704 the Frank, Duke Hetan II, and his wife Theodora documented a donation with the name of the location **"in Castello Virteburch."** Hetan was the last ruler in his dynasty, a fact that is rather closely connected to the **Kilian legend.** Gailana, the wife of Hetan I, married her brother-in-law Gosbert upon the death of her husband. The Irish missionary **Kilian** wanted this marriage annulled because according to Christian beliefs, the woman had married a relative. Gailana took the matter in her own hands and had

the market street. Around the year 1000, the first wall was erected. It ran along the Juliuspromenade, Theaterstrasse, Balthasar-Neumann-Promenade and Neubaustrasse and was shaped, more or less, like a **bishop's miter.** Nowadays the Old Town comprises this area. Further settlement and the development of monasteries outside the walls made it necessary to expand them in 1200. The city had a thriving **Jewish community** and its rabbis were renowned for their scholarship. Christians and Jews managed to live peacefully side-by-side but **pogroms** time and again, overshadowed the city and in 1298 and 1349 devastating persecutions destroyed the Jewish community entirely.

Power Conflicts

From early on, the bishops of Würzburg were successful religious leaders. Bishops became **prince-bishops**, which gave them the added benefit of exerting worldly power as well. The burghers were concerned about this double role and wanted to rule themselves. Wars were

Kilian and his two followers, **Totnan** and **Kolonat**, murdered in 689. She suffered a gruesome end herself and one generation later, the ducal family died out completely. The remains of the missionaries were later found in a horse stable and large groups of pilgrims were soon attracted to the **martyrs' reliquaries.** The city itself benefited from the **pilgrimages** and there were two major settlements in the early Middle Ages. The first was on the far side of the Main River, the **Old Main quarter,** in the shadow of the Marienberg; the second was on higher ground, the court of the Franks, where later the **Cathedral** was built.

In 742 **Boniface** founded the bishopric of Würzburg and named **Burkard** the first bishop. Just a few years after that, the first **Cathedral** was consecrated and new settlement increased on the right side of the river where the valley was wider. The **Domstrasse** (Dom = Cathedral) became both the main street and

Above: Matthäus Merian: copperplate etching of Würzburg with its medieval walls from around 1633.

"Herbipolis" – Würzburg, the City of Herbs

In the 7th century a geographer from Ravenna wrote a description of the world at that time. One of the places he mentioned was "Uburzis" or "Wurziburg." It is very probable that he meant Würzburg because other old names sound similar. Early on, the syllable "Würz," a form of the German for herbs or seasonings, was used in the Latin version "Herbipolis." This name is plausible since the vineyard slopes are known for their herbal varieties as well as their grapes.

fought over this predominance and repeatedly, the bishops maintained the upper hand. These religious men resided in the **Marienberg Fortress** whose walls were continually being reinforced. The first major conflict occurred in 1400 when **King Wenceslas** promised to make Würzburg a Free Imperial City. He never carried through with his promise, however, and a short time later, the townspeople attempted to seize power militarily and suffered a dramatic defeat just north of Würzburg at the **Battle of Bergtheim**. The final attempt to rule independently came during the **Peasants' War** in 1525 when the burghers sided with the peasants against the bishop's forces. This defeat was even bloodier.

Becoming a City with a Residence

The Reformation as well posed a threat to the predominance of the Catholic Church. In 1573, **Julius Ech-** **ter von Mespelbrunn**, an emphatic Counter-Reformer, became prince-bishop. He left an indelible mark by establishing the **Juliusspital Charitable Institution** and the **University**. Echter forced **Protestants** to leave the city and instigated **witch-hunts** that were horribly escalated under his successor Ehrenberg. After the **Swedes** besieged the Marienberg Fortress during the **Thirty Years' War**, Prince-bishop Johann Philipp Franz von Schönborn began making plans for completely new Baroque fortifications. **Baroque construction** flourished in the city in the 18th century as well and the culmination of this architecture was realized in the construction of the **Residence**, the new home of the prince-bishops.

Above: A copper etching depicting Würzburg after the construction of its Baroque bastions.
Right: George Clarkson Stanfield's 1876 oil painting of Kilian Fair near Neumünster Church.

Bavarian Franconians

The **bishopric** was dissolved in 1802/03 and Würzburg was annexed to the state of **Bavaria**. The city enjoyed a short intermezzo as the **Grand Duchy of Tuscany** but in 1814, integration to Bavaria was finalized. Although Franconians officially became Bavarians, they have managed to retain their unique mentality and regional dialects.

The real obstacle of further city development in the 19th century was the extensive Baroque fortifications that the state of Bavaria insisted on maintaining as city walls until 1856 and as fortress fortifications until 1867. The **Ring Park** replaced the city walls as of 1880 and this island of green has proven to be a bit of good luck. The University was also able to expand on some of the property. The city's expansion continued and in addition to the **Old Main Bridge**, the **Luitpold Bridge** and the **Ludwig Bridge** formed a vital link to the far side of the river. In 1930, the small village of **Heidingsfeld** was the first community to be incorporated into the city.

Resurrected from the Ruins

A disastrous turning point occurred on **March 16, 1945**, when the British Royal Air Force bombed out the Old Town. Five thousand people lost their lives. Würzburg was a sea of rubble, yet its inhabitants returned and started their lives anew. Apartment buildings were hastily constructed but more time and consideration went into the rebuilding of the city's historical monuments. The core of the Residence survived as well as innumerable works of art that had been stored in safety. Too much was irretrievable but the overall character of the city could be preserved. Street patterns were left unchanged and historic buildings rebuilt in their former architectural style.

Würzburg in the 21st Century

The city's economy is based on **medium-sized businesses**, in particular, publishing houses and high tech companies. Würzburg is an **administrative hub** and retail center. Koenig & Bauer High Speed Printing Machines and the Mero-TSK Steel Construction Company are two of the larger industries associated with the city. Approximately 25,000 students are enrolled in higher education at polytechnical institutes, the School of Music and the Julius-Maximilian University that is highly regarded for its School of Medicine and the biosciences.

Due to its favorable location and easy accessibility via rail or the autobahn, Würzburg is a popular **convention center** as well. Not to be forgotten is the city's broad cultural scene that offers something for everyone, be it the Africa Festival, the Mozart Festival or the Wine Village. Tasty Franconian culinary specialties as well as a wide selection of international cuisine ensure a hearty appetite.

Getting there

Autobahns A3, A7 and A81 have Würzburg exits; the **ICE train** makes frequent stops. The train station is centrally located and local public transportation is good. The **Frankfurt Airport** has a train every hour as well as autobahn connections to Würzburg. **Cyclists** will appreciate the bike route along the Main River. This is a good place to start becoming acquainted with the **Romantic Road**, a scenic and romantic route through southern Germany.

When to go

Popular times of the year include the spring and the fall as well as during the month of August when the state of Bavaria is on vacation. It is advisable to book hotel rooms in advance during peak seasons.

Facts & Figures

Population: 135,000
Downtown area: c. 180 meters above sea level
Frankenwarte: 360 meters above sea level

Würzburg lies in the heart of Franconian wine country. The Main River valley has a mild, average temperature of 18.3° Celsius in mid-July and the annual rainfall is 600 mm.

The City

Würzburg is the capital of the Bavarian administrative district of Lower Franconia. In addition to its numerous tourist sights, its important position offers fine shopping, good hospitals and a wide variety of dining possibilities as well as cultural events.

Downtown, City Quarters and Parks

The majority of sights and stores are located in the historical **Old Town** on the right side of the Main River inside the Ring Park or the Bishop's Miter which is bordered by the Juliuspromenade, Theaterstrasse and Balthasar-Neumann-Promenade. On the far side of the river is the **Old Main Quarter** and the Marienberg Fortress. **Zellerau, Sanderau** and **Grombühl** as well as Frauenland and the **university campus on Hubland** are the main quarters of the city.
The historical village of **Heidingsfeld** was incorporated in 1930 and a good thirty years later, **Heuchelhof** with its apartment high rises was constructed. The area now extends to Rottenbauer. Rottenbauer as well as Oberdürrbach, Unterdürrbach, Versbach and Lengfeld were incorporated in the 1970s. The city is fortunate

Left: Würzburg lies in a sea of rubble. Watercolor taken from the Old Main Bridge towards the Cathedral by Leo Dittmer in 1946.

to have a number of **green zones** such as the Ring Park, the Bavarian Garden Show Park and the vineyards on the slopes of the Marienberg, the famous Stein vineyards behind the train station and the Frankenwarte recreational area atop the hill behind the Käppele Pilgrimage Church.

Getting around

Würzburg is a small metropolis whose Old Town can be enjoyed as a pedestrian. There are numerous parking garages (fee) and the sights are well-signposted. Several north-south streetcar lines run regularly. Bus 9 takes the traveler from the Residence across town to the Granary Museum and then on to the Marienberg Fortress (seasonal) and bus 35 leaves from the Sanderring and goes to the Frankenwarte and the Käppele (year round). The traveler can also drive or walk to all these sights.

Famous Contemporaries

The basketball player, Dirk Nowitzki, and the cabaret artist, Frank-Markus Barwasser, were born in Würzburg. Peter Bofinger is a professor of economics at the university.

The Bridges and their Tricky Names

For some strange reason, all the bridges except the Old Main Bridge have at least two names. The following is an abbreviated guide:

Laurentius Bridge = Zeller Bridge

The Bridge of German Unity = Talavera Bridge

Luitpold Bridge = Peace Bridge

Konrad-Adenauer Bridge = South Bridge = Train Bridge = Heidingsfeld Bridge

Opening hours

Except for the Residence, most museums and sights are closed Mondays but the many **churches** are usually open to the public except during church services and mass. A brochure lists the hours of the church services. The **Cathedral**, however, has specific opening hours.

Don't miss

Sightseeing Tour 1

Begin at the **Old Main Bridge** ③, walk to the **Market Place to Mary's Chapel** ⑦ and to the **House to the Falcon** ⑥ that houses the Tourist Information Office. Next, walk to **Neumünster Church** ⑧ then to the **Cathedral** ②. Leave the Cathedral by a left side door and head to **Lusam Garden** ⑨ which is behind the choir of **Neumünster Church**. Then go down the Hofstrasse to the **Residence** ①. From there take bus 9 (seasonal) to the **Marienberg Fortress** ④ and the **Main-Franconian Museum**. Depart from here by bus or walk down the lovely path that ends on the far side of the Old Main Bridge. A separate trip is made to the Käppele ⑤. When the seasonal bus isn't running, it is advisable to

Above: Erich Heckel painted this view of Marienberg Fortress in 1927.
Right: A view of the Old Town with the Cathedral in the center.

make a separate trip to the Marienberg (see chapter on the Fortress).

Sightseeing Tour 2

This is for visitors with a minimum on time. Start at the **Old Main Bridge** ③ and enjoy the panoramic view of the **Old Town**, the **Marienberg Fortress** ④ and the **Käppele** ⑤. Walk the Domstrasse to **Neumünster Church** ⑧, the **Cathedral** ② and **Lusam Garden** ⑨. Then walk to the **Residence** ①.

Getting round
without knowing German

Würzburg prides itself not only on being a university town; it is also home to several polytechnic schools, colleges and other specialty institutes. This all means that the city is bustling and alive with young people who add a casual flair in the pedestrian zone as well as in the cafes. For this very reason, it is fairly easy to get around as a non-German speaking tourist whether it be asking directions or ordering in a café or restaurant. Young people will always speak some English.

Even basic German is no guarantee that you will understand or be understood since the Franconian dialect is difficult to pick up without some initial practice. Do not fret; northern Germans do not understand south Germans and vice-versa! High German is not necessarily a given in this region even though the city is a center of learning.

Taking the train involves purchasing a ticket from a vending machine in the train station prior to boarding. The system is rather complicated but click on the instructions in English for the best results. The exact change comes out with the ticket.

The Palace of Palaces

UNESCO-World Heritage Site

Synthesis of the arts in 340 rooms

Giovanni Battista Tiepolo's

renowned ceiling fresco –

Cabinet of Mirrors –

Mozart Festival

and State Court Cellars

Left: View of the Court Gardens from the south wing of the Residence.

Above: The painter, Mattias Grünewald, at the Franconia Fountain in the Residence square.

The Residence in Würzburg

Contemporaries named it the "palace of palaces," Napoleon called it the "loveliest parsonage in Europe" and the UNESCO made it a world heritage site in 1981. Small wonder the Residence has so many admirers. This is where the leading artisans in Europe collaborated to create a synthesis of the arts. A by-product of this creation was the birth of Würzburg Rococo.

The History of its Construction

In 1683 the Cathedral canon had already decided that the bishop should move from the fortress into the city. **Antonio Petrini** erected a small castle but it was never inhabited. It was literally built on sand. The **Rosenbach Palace** to the north of the Residence is all that is left of his original construction. No one was willing to move in until **Johann Philipp Franz von Schönborn** became prince-bishop and a successful court case awarded him an enormous sum of money. The prince-bishop found himself with enough funds to support his infamous "building mania." And the cornerstone of a new Residence was laid in 1720. A young, inexperienced architect by the name of **Balthasar Neumann** was commissioned not only to satisfy the wishes of the Schönborn family; moreover, he had to work together with the architectural

Don't miss

1. Ceiling Fresco by Giovanni Battista Tiepolo
2. Imperial Hall
3. Cabinet of Mirrors
4. Court Chapel
5. Martin-von-Wagner Museum
6. State Court Cellars
7. Court Gardens

learned how to implement his own plans. In 1724, **Christoph Franz von Hutten** became prince-bishop and his lackluster interest in the project allowed the north block to be completed but nothing more. It wasn't until 1729 under Prince-bishop **Friedrich Karl von Schönborn** that construction once again began. The shell of the Residence was completed in 1744 but another interruption occurred until **Carl Philipp von Greiffenclau** became prince-bishop and arranged for the decoration of the interior. The interior design was not completed until 1781 when the small bishopric of Würzburg found itself with a castle of European dimensions. The fame was short-lived as in 1802/03 secularization dissolved the bishopric and annexed the city over to the Bavarian government that turned the Residence into a secondary palace for the Bavarian kings.

elite of the period. **Maximilian von Welsch** from Mainz, **Johann Lucas von Hildebrandt** from Vienna, and the Frenchmen, **Robert de Cotte** and **Germain Boffrand**, were called in as consultants and advisors. Nonetheless, Neumann alone was in charge of the construction and he quickly

Above: The garden view of the Residence with its prominent Imperial Hall in the center.
Following pages: The Franconia Fountain wasn't erected until 1894.

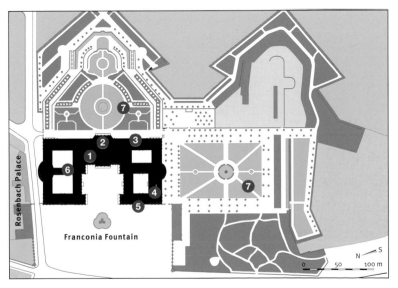

Rosenbach Palace

Franconia Fountain

0   50   100 m

The first **Mozart Festival** was held in 1922 and ever since the music of Mozart is synonymous with the Residence's atmospheric interior and its Court Gardens. Although the Residence wasn't spared during the bombing on **March 16, 1945**, the vaulted ceilings in the central complex held firm and the exquisite ceiling frescos could be salvaged. An American officer, **John D. Skilton**, was put in charge of rescuing works of art and he quickly had a protective roof installed. A portion of the furnishings had been removed for safekeeping. The extensive **reconstruction** was completed in 1987. The preservation and maintenance of the Residence continues as a lifelong process.

Visiting the Residence

An individual tour of the Residence begins on the ground floor and continues up the **Grand Staircase ①** to the **Imperial Hall ②**. A guided tour includes the Imperial

1. Vestibule
2. Garden Salon
3. Grand Staircase
4. White Salon
5. Imperial Hall
6. South Wing Apartments
7. Cabinet of Mirrors
8. Gallery
9. Servants' Quarters
10. North Wing Apartment
11. Green Lacquered Room
12. Bavarian State Gallery
13. Ingelheim Staterooms
14. Blue Room
15. Salon of Princes
16. Court Church

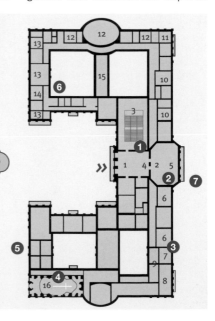

Apartments and the **Cabinet of Mirrors** ❸. The **Court Church** ❹, accessible from the square, is located at the southern end of the complex. The wrought iron gate adjacent leads into the **Court Gardens** ❼. The **Martin-von-Wagner Museum** ❺ is also located in the south wing. A tour of the **Court Cellars** ❻ beneath the Residence is also recommended.

The Hofgarten or Court Gardens ❼

Open daily until dusk; free

The Court Gardens were not begun until the Residence had been completed. Land was limited to the east between the main garden and the bastions. However, more space was available to the south. In 1770, Prince-bishop **Adam Friedrich von Seinsheim** commissioned the Bohemian landscape gardener, **Johann Prokop Mayer**, to create an elegant, more diversified Rococo Garden even though English landscape gardening was en vogue. The east garden was built like an amphitheater with terraces, staircases, ramps and bowers that cleverly disguised the bastion. The prince-bishop also had plans for a large cascade which due to his death in 1779 were never realized. The landscape gardener, Johann Demeter, designed a central basin as the focal point of the south gardens which formed a lateral axis to the Residence. The **orangery** was located at the far end. The early Classical statues, putti angels, urns and fauns as well as two groups of statues, the **Rape of Europe** and the **Rape of Proserpine** were from the workshop of **Peter Wagner.**

Above left and middle: Peter Wagner and his workshop created the numerous playful figures and statues that adorn the Court Gardens. Above: Balthasar Neumann constructed the Residence at the edge of the city inside the bastions.

Franz Ludwig von Erthal, a parsimonious prince-bishop, buried Mayer's grandiose plans in 1779 and settled instead for a natural garden in the southwest. Mayer was opposed to such a "new-fangled" wilderness, but the prince-bishop had his way.

Residenzplatz 2
Tel.: 0931 / 355170

Apr – Oct: daily 9 – 18
Nov – March: daily 10 – 16:30
(Last entry: 30 minutes before closing)
(Guided tours in English daily at 11 & 15)

www.residenz-wuerzburg.de

The ornate rooms in the **corps de logis** of the central building leave a theatrical impression that is dramatized by alternating simple plain

walls with gloriously painted fresco ceilings.

The Vestibule

The rather low ceiling of the vestibule is supported by muscular **Atlantes** created by **Wolfgang van der Auvera. Franz Anton Ermeltraut's** ceilings appropriately retell the deeds of Hercules. **Lodovico Bossi** was responsible for the decorative stuccowork while **Peter Wagner** designed the marble statues. The vestibule was designed to permit horse-drawn carriages to enter and turn around inside in inclement weather.

Above: The renowned Grand Staircase in the Residence.

The Grand Staircase ❶

The more important the guest, the further down the staircase the prince-bishop came. The flat steps enabled the visitor to glide upwards, each step revealing more of the overpowering ostentation of the magnificent reception room. The view is at first focused on the allegorical figures designed by the sculptor, **Peter Wagner**, on the balustrade. Only then does the significance of the architecture make itself manifest. The Grand Staircase is crowned by a vaulted ceiling 18 by 30 meters in size constructed without any support whatsoever. Legend has it that during construction, Neumann had a cannonball fired to dispel any doubts concerning the stability of the structure. The real test came when the ceiling survived the bombing attacks of the Second World War.

No one was more qualified to paint the huge ceiling than the Venetian, **Giovanni Battista Tiepolo**, who completed a fresco nearly 600 m² in size between 1752/53. Each of the four known continents **Europe, Asia, Africa and America** were personified by a princess. Australia was not yet represented. Factual knowledge was heavily influenced by fanciful impressions that never fail to amaze. To the north, a page is serving Princess America hot chocolate while a well-hidden European watches an act of cannibalism.

Trade played an important role in the depiction of Africa to the east. One scene shows a monkey ripping out an ostrich's tail feathers. Nile, the river deity, sits in a corner. Note how his plaster leg extends from the fresco.

Asia is characterized by Golgotha or Calvary and an Egyptian pyramid. Tiepolo made a small stone

plaque bearing his name and dated 1753. Asia is not exactly portrayed in the best light: bound slaves are depicted writhing in pain.

These side frescos are united by a celestial gathering of the dei-

Left: Giovanni Battista Tiepolo painted the 18 x 30 meter fresco on the vault above the Grand Staircase.

Above: Africa, America and Asia pay tribute to the prince-bishop.

ties, the most important of whom is Apollo, the Sun god himself and the god of the arts.

Fanciful personifications representing the planets pay tribute to the patron prince-bishop. Heaven and earth are both present here without a trace of a Christian element.

Upon reaching the landing, Europe comes into view portrayed as an assembly of the sciences and the arts. A **medallion** with the portrait of Prince-bishop Carl Philipp von Greiffenclau is positioned in the clouds overhead. **Balthasar Neumann** in uniform is seated on top of a cannon. In the left corner **Tiepolo** has painted himself wearing a be-

Top: Europe is depicted as the synthesis of the arts and sciences.

Above: Self-portrait of Tiepolo in the vault.

Right: Balthasar Neumann wearing a Franconian colonel's uniform.

Balthasar Neumann
(1687-1753)

*The son of a cloth maker from a large family, Neumann worked his way to the top. He completed an apprenticeship as a founder in his hometown of Eger, Bohemia, and arrived in Würzburg in 1711. He joined the Franconian District Artillery and became acquainted with the military captain, Andreas Müller, who recognized Neumann's capabilities. In 1719 Neumann, a military captain as well, was commissioned to plan and oversee the construction of the **Residence**. In his spare time, Neumann created numerous other edifices in the city such as **Schönborn Chapel**, the **Machicolation Tower***

*at the Marienberg, the **department store** on the Market Square, **Marmelsteiner Hof** and the **Käppele Pilgrimage Church**. The **Oberzell convent**, the garden pavilion in Randersacker, and the **churches** in Gaibach, Kitzingen and in Werneck Castle are some examples of his work in Lower Franconia. The **Grand Staircase** in Brühler Castle, the **Augustusburg** and **Vierzehnheiligen Pilgrimage Church** pay testimony to his versatility.*
Neumann is largely responsible for the layout of the Baroque city of Würzburg and for the flow of running water from its fountains.
*A plaque in Mary's Chapel marks his **burial place**.*

ret; his son, **Giovanni Domenico,** in a white wig, is seated next to him.

The White Salon

Würzburg Rococo has been called the most lively and high-spirited example of Rococo in Germany. It exemplifies the combined efforts of architects, artists, master craftsmen, stone fitters and sculptors such as Wolfgang van der Auvera and master plasterer, **Antonio Bossi**. At first glance the room appears anything but lavish. White dominates alongside a pale gray and every now and then, a dab of light yellow shines through. The Salon's grandeur is celebrated in Bossi's use of intricate almost intimate rocaille plasterwork which produces a magnificent effect in contrast to the brown wood of the doors. The fine lines of the flamboyant rocaille ensemble with its martial emblems do not appear the slightest bit matte or lifeless. They are fitting to their impressive, powerfully monumental dimensions. It is hard to believe that this room was originally a guardroom. Schönborn Chapel, the final resting place of the Schönborn prince-bishops, can be seen from the windows.

The Imperial Hall ❷

The Imperial Hall and its adjoining Imperial Apartments were part and parcel of Baroque palaces and charitable institutions, especially when the future emperor happened to be passing through on his way to being crowned in Frankfurt. Würzburg was one of the future emperor's stopovers and upon the prince-bishop's instructions, **Tiepolo** celebrated this visit in the Imperial Hall by placing his emphasis on the Holy Roman Empire. The frescos evoke Würzburg motifs from the annals

of the Hohenstaufen Empire mysteriously blended in with mythical figures.

Tiepolo created three large ceiling frescos for this hall. At one end, **Frederick Barbarossa** confers the Franconian ducal title on Bishop Herold; at the opposite end, Frederick Barbarossa weds **Beatrice of Burgundy**. Tiepolo's choice of subject matter was no accident. The bishop of Würzburg administered the holy vows in 1156 symbolizing his service to both the emperor and the empire. In 1168, the emperor demonstrated his approval of the legitimacy of the reign of the prince-bishop. This was a topic that had grown in importance in the 18th century since there was already talk of dissolving the outdated bishoprics. Tiepolo's frescos elevated the use of painting to serve politics. As a well paid Venetian master of his trade, Tiepolo was given free rein in his portrayals. A closer study reveals numerous whimsical scenes that are almost

Left: The Imperial Hall offers the ideal venue for concerts during the Mozart Festival.
Above: Side fresco in the Imperial Hall portraying the bishop receiving the Franconian ducal title.

caricature-like: the upside down bishop's miter or the facial features of Prince-bishop **Greiffenclau** at the Imperial wedding. The ceiling itself is a variation on the wedding theme and is titled **"The Sun God Brings Beatrice of Burgundy to the Genius Imperii."**

The frescos above the doors, exemplary scenes from the lives of former emperors, were painted by **Giovanni Domenico**, who along with his brother **Lorenzo** had accompanied their father on this commission. **Antonio Bossi** designed the large plasterwork figures of Neptune, Juno, Flora and Apollo in the corners.

Twenty red-white marbled stucco half columns almost nine meters tall line the walls. A glance out the windows offers a superb view of the lush Court Gardens.

Home of the Mozart Festival

As **Hermann Zilcher** conducted Mozart for the first time in the Imperial Hall in 1921, he felt at once that Würzburg should have a Mozart Festival and that this hall was the perfect venue: "It seemed to me as if all at once the figures and statues, all

the frescos came alive; I merely had to allow my conductor's baton to follow the contours of the ornamentation and an internal marriage took place among music, architecture and color...".

A year later, Zilcher opened the first official **Mozart Festival** and it has long since become an annual musical event in the Imperial Hall, White Salon and in the Court Gardens. The thickets and bowers, stairs and foliage, and balustrades and lanterns in the gardens at dusk on a warm summer evening offer a unique experience.

The Imperial Apartments

The length of the Residence becomes evident when all the doors of the Imperial Apartments to the north and south of the Imperial Hall stand open: the view extends 160 meters.

Imperial Apartments were common in residences in southern Germany. These lavishly decorated rooms were guest apartments for the occasional sojourn of an emperor or other noble guest. The apartments in the side wings were more heavily damaged than the central building and much of the furnishing was irretrievable. Many period pieces now on display are not originally from the Residence.

The **apartments in the south wing** were completed between 1740 and 1744 during the reign of **Friedrich Carl von Schönborn** who relied on renowned artisans. Most of the wainscoting and woodcarvings are original and the gold hues add war-

Left: The sumptuous Cabinet of Mirrors at the end of the south wing apartments.
Above: The Blue Antechamber is one of the Ingelheim Staterooms.

mth to the décor. The functional **antechamber** leads into the **audience chamber** and on to the **Venetian chamber**. This room was designated for the emperor and is adorned with small 18th century masterpieces.

The **Cabinet of Mirrors ❸** was recreated from a single shard of glass that served as a model for the entire room. Photographs and special technology were used to gild and lacquer the glass from the back. From 1979-1987 **Wolfgang Lenz**, a local painter, based his work on the sketches of Wolfgang van der Auvera. The restoration is a masterpiece of exuberant splendor. **Antonio Bossi's** stuccowork in the corner vaults once again depicts the allegorical figures of the four known continents.

The rooms in the gallery are decorated in the manner of **Grand Duke Ferdinand III of Tuscany.** In 1806, Ferdinand III, a Hapsburg, received the former bishopric of Würzburg as compensation for Tuscany that

he had previously ruled. He had the so-called **Tuscany Room** decorated in the popular Empire style of the era. He also brought along his art gallery that filled three rooms. His reign ended in 1814 when he got Tuscany back and Würzburg's annexation to Bavaria could then be finalized.

A stroll through the servants' quarters leads back to the central tract. It is here that the tile ovens that heated the rooms were stoked. Inconspicuous tapestry doors lead directly into the apartments.

North Wing Apartments

Prince-bishop **Friedrich Carl von Schönborn** was also responsible for the furnishings in the north wing of the Imperial Apartments. His successor, **Carl Philipp von**

Above: Large tapestries with scenes from the life of Alexander the Great.
Right: The resplendent Green Lacquered Room.

Greiffenclau, had the first four rooms sumptuously refurbished between 1749 and 1754.

The **Napoleonic Stateroom** was the room that **Emperor Napoleon** slept in when he was in Würzburg. Between 1806 and 1813 he stopped in the city three times; like France, it was a member of the Confederation of the Rhine. The further north the visitor walks, the later the decorative style. The last three rooms which were furnished after 1763 were strongly influenced by Louis 16th. The **Green Lacquer Room** at the corner is a blend of Würzburg Rococo and early Classicism. The amazing reconstructed parquet flooring is a maze of optical illusions.

Bavarian State Gallery

The State Art Gallery occupies the rooms facing north. The collection includes 17th and 18th century Venetian paintings appropriate to the

epoch of the Residence. Tiepolo's ceiling paintings were the motivation behind the collection. The **Oval Salon** is a part of the State Gallery and its unusual acoustics pay tribute to the days when this was an opera hall.

Ingelheim Staterooms

These staterooms were named after Prince-bishop **Anselm Franz von Ingelheim** who resided here from 1746-1749. The furnishings from the 1770s are considered exquisite examples of early Classicism in Germany and postdate him.

Salon of Princes

Named in honor of eight portraits of prince-bishops including **Adam Friedrich von Seinsheim** who began this enormous project, this room as well was heavily influenced by early Classicism. The salon has served as a concert hall, reception hall and dining room. Court guests al-

so gathered here to chat and play games.

Garden Salon

Balthasar Neumann had an original idea for this room on the ground floor: twelve freestanding slender marble columns support the vaulted ceiling that resembles a cloth baldachin. **Antonio Bossi's** light blue plasterwork enhances the sala terrena's airy gracefulness. **Johann Zick's** ceiling painting from 1750 is in juxtaposition to the ensemble: he chose dark, earthy hues to portray his **Feast of the Gods** and **Diana's Repose**.

Court Church ❹

Apr – Oct: daily 9 – 18
Nov – Mar: daily 10 – 16:30
The church is closed during mass and for weddings
Free

Neumann inconspicuously incorporated the Court Church into the southwest corner of the Residence without disturbing the symmetry of the composition. Only the steps leading up to the church doors give an indication of something irregular. Neumann's architectural concept of fitting Rococo oval vaults,

Above: Oval vaults, lunettes and galleries contribute to the lavish splendor in the Court Church.
Left: The Garden Salon on the ground floor.

lunettes and galleries into a rectangular outer shell was a part of the chapel's brilliance. However, the history of the chapel's planning was long and marked with vicissitudes. In the end, Neumann did manage to carry out his entire concept; he commissioned the renowned **Rudolph Byss** and his workshop to paint the "secco" ceilings that did not survive the war and Antonio Bossi to carry out the stuccowork. **Wolfgang van der Auvera** was responsible for the statues of St. Kilian and St. Burkard at the High Altar. He commissioned Italian sculptors to carve from the finest Carrara marble. **Tiepolo** also contributed his skills by creating the Fall of the Angels and the Assumption, two large paintings for the side altars.

The result is one of the most perfect religious edifices of the 18th century.

Martin-von-Wagner Museum ❺

Residenzplatz 2
Tel.: 0931 / 312288

Tues – Sat 10 – 13:30 (Art Gallery)
13:30 – 17 (Classical Antiquities Gallery)
Tues, Thurs 16 – 18 and by appointment
(Graphic Arts Collection)
Sun 10 – 13:30 (Art Gallery, Classical
Antiquities Gallery)
Topical guided tours from time to time
www.uni-wuerzburg.de/museum

Martin von Wagner, the son of the court sculptor, **Peter Wagner,** was an artist and art collector for **Ludwig I.** He donated his private collection to the university in Würzburg. The museum is located in the south wing and consists of three individual galleries.

The **Classical Antiquity Collection** boasts the third largest collection of Greek vases in Germany.

The **Egyptian Collection** contains over 300 artifacts and is definitely worth seeing. Other rooms display artifacts from the Near East, Cyprus and Italy.

The **Art Gallery** features German, Dutch and Italian paintings and works of art from the 14th to the 20th century. Many of the exhibits are from the private collection of Martin von Wagner.

The **Graphic Arts Collection** has tens of thousands of drawings and prints. There are 3,000 sheets from the Italian Renaissance and Baroque painters and 120 drawings by **Tiepolo** and **his sons. Peter Wagner,** the court artist in Würzburg, is represented here alongside such great names as **Altdorfer, Dürer, Cranach and Brueghel.**

Left: An exquisite Greek vase from the Classical Antiquities Collection.

Above: Portrait of a female in the Classical antiquity style.

Right: A fragment of Classical grace.

Court Cellars ⑥
Residenzplatz 3
Tel.: 0931 / 3050923

Open only in connection with a guide or special events
Guided tour (seasonal):
Sat, Sun, holidays 10, 11, 12, 14, 15 & 16;
Sat 17 as well
Meeting point: Franconia Fountain on the Residence Square
www.hofkeller.de

Upon commissioning **Balthasar Neumann** to build the Residence, Prince-bishop **Johann Philipp Franz von Schönborn** expressed his desire for an "excellent wine cellar". This cellar beneath the Residence was so exceptional that it is still in use. Already while descending down the stones steps, the unique atmosphere of these huge old vaulted cellars becomes evident. The walls are up to six meters thick and 600,000 liters of wine are fermenting and aging in the **wooden barrels** alone. But that is only half

the story. The approximately 900 meter long corridors connect the larger with the smaller rooms. Note the **"civil servant" barrels** which were reserved for the court civil servants as a liquid salary. In addition to the regular guided tours, there are **wine tastings** that are often in conjunction with special culinary themes. Occasionally, the vaulted cellars serve as a concert hall and cinema theater.

The state-run Court Cellars, formerly the prince-bishops' court cellars, look back on an 875-year old history. The Court Cellars is one of the three traditional Franconian wineries with 120 hectares of vineyards. Renowned appellations such as Innere Leiste are a given. A highlight of wine tasting occurs each year at the end of June when the Residence turns its gardens into a **Court Garden Fest.**

Purchasing Wine in Rosenbach Palace Residenzplatz 3,
(at the north end of the Square)
Tel: 0931/3050923
Mon – Fri 9 - 18, Sat 9 - 14

Left and above: Wine has been aging here for hundreds of years. Festive candlelight reveals that many of the old wooden barrels are beautifully carved works of art.

St. Kilian's Cathedral and Neumünster Church

Romanesque, Baroque and Modern –
Kilian's Crypt and the Cathedral Crypt –
Riemenschneider's Effigies –
Lusam Garden and
Walther von der Vogelweide –
Works of Art

Left: The curvilinear west façade of Neumünster Church; the entrance to Kilian's Crypt is beneath the undulating double staircase.
Above: Statues of the three Franconian apostles Kilian, Kolonat and Totnan in Neumünster Church.

In the Cathedral Quarter

Scholars still debate whether the first Cathedral was built on the site of the Neumünster Church or the site where the present Cathedral stands. Everyone agrees that the Cathedral quarter was the center of the city on the right side of the river and not in the flood zone. It has been documented that Bishop Burkard had a wooden Cathedral erected here in 755 and had the relics of the Franconian apostle Kilian transferred to the crypt. Charlemagne attended the consecration of the first stone Cathedral in 788.

Neumünster Church
Kürschnerhof 2½

The basilica was begun in the 11th century and the Romanesque core of the structure can still be seen from the front. In the 16th century the north spire was added and in 1614 the vaulted Baroque ceiling was begun. Joseph Greising created two architectural masterpieces: the pentagonal dome that literally crowns this house of worship and the concave Baroque **west façade ❷**. Greising may have based his work on a plan from **Johann Dientzenhofer.** The sculpture work, carried out by **Jacob van der Auvera**, depicts Christ the Savior in the middle flanked by

Don't miss

❶ *Effigy for Rudolf von Scherenberg*

❷ *Baroque west façade - Neumünster Church*

❸ *Lusam Garden*

❹ *Kilian's Crypt - Neumünster Church*

❺ *Cathedral Cloister*

❻ *Cathedral Treasury - Marmelsteiner Hof*

❼ *Museum at the Cathedral*

❽ *Crucifix of a bearded Christ - Cathedral Crypt*

❾ *Schönborn Chapel – Cathedral*

Burkard and Kilian and his fellow apostles.

Behind the altar in the sanctuary is a further portrayal of the Franconian apostles. The original busts by **Tilman Riemenschneider** were destroyed in 1945; fortunately, **Heinz Schiestl** had already made copies in 1910. The large stone **Madonna** and the **effigy** of Johannes Trithemius in the south entryway are also said to

be the works of Riemenschneider. Noteworthy is the 14th century **Crucifixion** depicting Christ with his arms folded.

Kilian's Crypt ❹ has always played

Left: The airy stuccowork enhances the vivid ceiling frescos in Neumünster Church.

Above: Lusam Garden behind Neumünster Church is an oasis of peace and quiet in the center of the city.

In the Cathedral Quarter **45**

an important role in the life of this church. The early Gothic Kilian's Altar with the modern bronze Kilian's reliquary contains the relics of the Franconian martyr except for the skull which is kept in the High Altar of the Cathedral.

Lusam Garden ❸
Entrance from the left side door of the church or from Martinstrasse

Open daily

This is a cool, quiet oasis of green hidden away behind the Neumünster Church. Only one side of a **Romanesque cloister** decorated with two finely-carved reliefs dating back to 1180 still remains. This is considered to be a prime example of the Hohenstaufen era in Würzburg. This garden is also said to be the final resting place of the minnesinger, **Walther von der Vogelweide. Frederick II** bestowed upon him an ecclesiastical benefice which allowed the

minnesinger to spend his later days without any financial worries. The poet died in 1230 and the plaque from 1930 is in remembrance of his sharp-tongued verse as well as his love poems.

TIP: *"Walter von der Vogelweide ante portas"* – Recitations, lieder, historical costumes and instruments
Tel: 09367/988680
Apr – Oct: 1ˢᵗ and 3ʳᵈ Sat at 16

St. Kilian's Cathedral
Domstrasse 42
Tel: 0931/3211830 (Cathedral parish)

Open: Mon – Sat 10 – 17,
Sun and holidays 13 – 18
Guided tours: Sun and holidays at 12:30;
Easter Mon to All Saints' Day;
additionally Mon – Sat 12:20
(organ music at 12:05)
www.dom-wuerzburg.de

Construction
The Cathedral dedicated to St. Kilian, the Franconian apostle, had several predecessors: a fire destroyed the building that either stood here or where the Neumünster Church now stands in 855. Bishop **Arno** had a larger Cathedral built in 918 but it burned as well. The next reconstruction is said to have taken until 940. In 1040 bishop **Bruno** laid the foundation stone for the present Cathedral which was consecrated in 1188. At the time, the Cathedral was considered huge and during the Hohenstaufen era, it doubled as a meeting place for Imperial Diets.

Left: The sanctuary of the Cathedral boasts several architectural styles.
Above: The mysterious cross with the bearded man in the Cathedral Crypt.

what this stuccowork was like. The Cathedral completely burned out on March 16, 1945, and its reconstruction was controversial but the decision was taken to incorporate several of the architectural styles that had survived and complement these styles with 20th century concepts. The plain outer façade was fashioned after a Romanesque basilica and on the **west façade** a neo-Romanesque rose window and gallery as well as a clock were incorporated into the stone facing. It wasn't until recently that these elements were discovered and uncovered.

Sanctuary

Entering the Cathedral from the main entrance, the visitor passes through a **wrought iron gate** which originally separated the choir from the congregation. A modern **menorah** symbolizes the Old Testament. This Cathedral was the prince-bishops' main church and it is exceptionally rich in religious artifacts such as the baptistery chapel on the right. Two unusual 13th century knotted **pillars** that were rescued from the narthex when it was being torn down in 1644 flank the entrance. **Master Eckard** from Worms cast the **baptismal** inside the chapel from a single piece of bronze in 1279. Its eight reliefs retell of God's saving grace. A 13th century interpretation of the **Holy Trinity** with the Virgin Mary is depicted on the columns on the north side of the nave. **Michael Kern** created the chalice-shaped **pulpit** in 1609. The **stone effigies** of various prince-bishops have to be considered the culmination of the Cathedral's treasures that begins with the oldest effigy on the left side of the nave. This is **Gottfried von Spitzberg** who died on a Crusade to Antioch in 1190. Cattycorner to him is **Otto**

At the beginning of the 17th century, vaulted ceilings were added in the sanctuary and in 1699, the entire interior was redesigned in the Baroque style. The Milanese master, **Pietro Magno**, worked on the plasterwork until 1705. The transept offers the visitor an impression of von **Wolfskeel's** memorial, a 14th century masterpiece of the Gothic by an anonymous sculptor. **Tilman Riemenschneider's** effigies of **Rudolf von Scherenberg ❶** and his successor, **Lorenz von Bibra**, on the left side of the nave are of exquisite quality. Scherenberg was around 65 when he was elected bishop in 1466. His successful and energetic reign lasted until his death in 1495.

Riemenschneider succeeded in creating an impressive portrayal of this venerated ruler. Riemenschneider's change in style in the two effigies is worth noting. While the older effigy is pure Gothic in style, it is clear that Riemenschneider is grappling with the Renaissance style in Bibra's effigy.

Schönborn Chapel ❾

The Schönborn Chapel completed in 1736 was, for the greatest part, based on **Balthasar Neumann's** design. It was well positioned on the north side of the transept within view of the Residence; its admonishing skulls and crossbones point

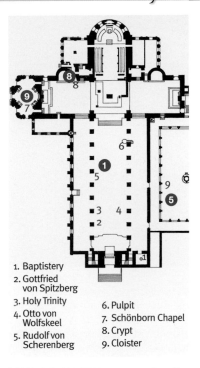

1. Baptistery
2. Gottfried von Spitzberg
3. Holy Trinity
4. Otto von Wolfskeel
5. Rudolf von Scherenberg
6. Pulpit
7. Schönborn Chapel
8. Crypt
9. Cloister

Left: Rudolf von Scherenberg's moving effigy was the skillful work of T. Riemenschneider.

Below: A 13th century baptismal in the baptistery.

to the fact that it was conceived as the final resting place of the Schönborn family. Access is by guided tour only but a glimpse through **Johannes Georg Oegg's** wrought iron gate reveals much of the chapel's splendor.

Crypt

The entrance to the Romanesque crypt lies between the Schönborn Chapel and the choir. **Bishop Bruno,** the founder of this Cathedral, lies buried here. **Balthasar Neumann** designed the crypt in 1749 with a low vault so that the choir above it could be lowered. Twelfth century **fresco wall fragments** portraying Christ in a mandorla have been rediscovered. Even older is the simple, but moving **Crucifix of a Bearded Christ** 8.

> **TIP:** A visitor's forum and information stand is located in the sanctuary daily until 17:00.

Above: Numerous effigies of laymen and clerics line the walls of the Cathedral cloister.
Right: View of the Cathedral cloister and its east spires.

Cloister ❺

An exit from the right side of the transept leads to the late Gothic cloister
where numerous effigies of mem-
bers of the Cathedral Chapter, vicars
and noble laymen line the walls.

Treasury ❻

Plattnerstrasse
Tel.: 09 31 / 38 66-56 00

Tues – Sun and holidays 14 – 17
**www.museen.bistum-wuerzburg.de/
domschatz**

Balthasar Neumann designed this
inconspicuous secular building, the
Marmelsteiner Hof, which houses
the exhibits a few steps south of the
Cathedral. The Treasury contains a
considerable number of vestments,
liturgical artifacts and gold work cov-
ering ten centuries. Organ music from
the Cathedral or an impressive light
show enhances these religious works
of art.

Museum at the Cathedral ❼

Kiliansplatz
Tel.: 09 31 / 3 86 65-6 00

Tues – Sun and holidays 10 - 18
(Nov – 31 March until 17)
www.museum-am-dom.de

A new museum on **Kilian Square**
between Neumünster Church and the
Cathedral opened its doors in 2003. Its

unusual concept is not to exhibit works of art dating from the 10th to the 21st centuries chronologically or according to an artistic genre. Instead, the museum bases its displays on a particular theme or pastoral message. It is fascinating to see works of art spanning the centuries standing in close proximity, each interpreting a similar topic in an equally similar or extremely dissimilar manner.

The collection includes works by **Tilman Riemenschneider** and Peter Wagner as well as paintings, ceramics and sculptures by **Otto Dix, Pablo Picasso, Joseph Beuys, Albrecht Dürer and Käthe Kollwitz.** The museum is augmented by regular temporary exhibits.

Hof Conti
Kardinal-Döpfner-Platz 4

The spiritual quarter of the Old Town between the Cathedral and the Residence boasted a number of Cathedral canons and noble palaces. Originally each of the 22 canons and vicars had their own private chapel. Hof Conti built by one of Julius Echter's nephews stands at the end of a narrow lane cattycorner from Schönborn Chapel; it features a high dome gable and a richly

decorated Renaissance oriel, both out of striking red sandstone. **Michael Kern** designed the alabaster altar in the private chapel which is not open to the public since nowadays this serves as the **Bishop of Würzburg's palace.**

Left: Schönborn chapel features skulls and crossbones that decoratively admonish the passerby; here lie the Schönborn prince-bishops.
Above: The sumptuous oriel of Hof Conti.

In the Heart of the Old Town

*Old Main Bridge and Bishop's Miter –
a proud Town Hall –
Farmer's Market in front of Mary's
Chapel – ornate Rococo on the
House to the Falcon –
where the peasants met during the
Peasants' War – drinking wine for
charity: the charitable institutions*

*Left: A mystical view from the Old Main Bridge into the Dom-
strasse.*
*Above: Baroque statues of saints flank the Old Main
Bridge.*

Where the locals enjoy life

The historic Old Town offers a variety of things to do aside from shopping. The number of sights is astounding for a town of this size, and cafes and cappuccino bars, restaurants and local wine inns are in abundance. Have a seat at an outdoor café or restaurant in the pedestrian zone and enjoy some people-watching.

Sightseeing Recommendation

Start at the **Old Main Bridge ❶**. The **Town Hall ❼** and **Vierröhren Fountain ❼** are adjacent. **Mary's Chapel ❸** and the **House to the Falcon ❷** are at the Market Place nearby. From the **Market Place,** the Marktgasse leads to the **Stachel Wine Inn ❾** with its unusual morning star hanging at the corner of Gressengasse. The Marktgasse also leads to the **Main River** and the **Old Crane ❽**. The next stop is the **Juliusspital**

Above: View from the Old Main Bridge past the Town Hall to the Cathedral.

Don't miss

❶ *Old Main Bridge*

❷ *House to the Falcon*

❸ *Mary's Chapel*

❹ *Town Hall*

❺ *Juliusspital Charitable Institution*

❻ *Stift Haug Church*

❼ *Vierröhren Fountain*

❽ *Old Crane*

❾ *Stachel Wine Inn*

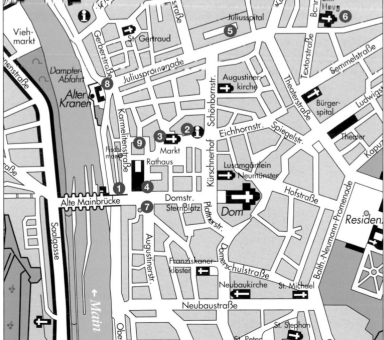

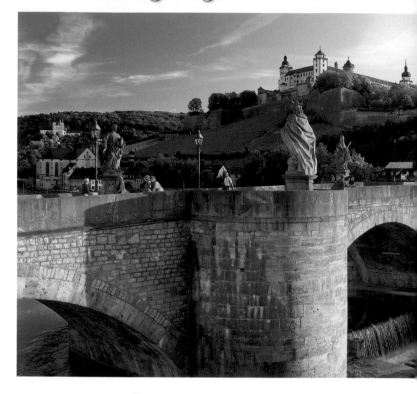

Charitable Institution ❺ on the Juliuspromenade and beyond is the **Stift Haug Church ❻**. This longer walk can be shortened by omitting either the Stift Haug Church ❻ or the Old Crane ❽.

> **TIP:** *Old Town guided tours in English begin at the House to the Falcon (see Practical Info section).*

A Burghers' Town Develops into a City

Both the **Cathedral** and **Neumünster Church** document the significant role of the Catholic Church in the history of Würzburg. At the same time they delineate the religious and secular trends that are still evident today. The life of the town's burghers and craftsmen, their living quarters and shops ex-

tend from these churches to the Main River. Shops and markets established themselves along the central axis of the **Domstrasse** until an unpleasant occurrence in the 15th century turned the **Market Place** into the focal point. At the end of the 19th century a new north-south axis connected the train station to the Cathedral. The creation of a **pedestrian zone** was a further logical consequence in this busy town.

> **TIP:** *Lovely specialty shops and local family-run shops are located on the narrower side streets to the left and the right of the main shopping area.*

The Old Main Bridge ❶

Even a short visit to Würzburg would not be complete without having crossed the Old Main Bridge with its

es and a chapel were a part of the gates. The Baroque **stone statues** were added in the 18th century. The saints on the south side are closely related to the town: the **Virgin Mary,** the patron saint of Franconia, is the sole female statue. She is surrounded by the Franconian saints **Kilian, Kolonat** and **Totnan. Burkard**, the first bishop of Würzburg, and **Bruno** who had the Cathedral built are also represented. More saints and rulers adorn the north side.

TIP: *The Alte Mainmühle Restaurant at the end of the bridge offers light and hearty fare as well as fine dining. The view of the Marienberg from the balcony is splendid (Alte Mainmühle, Mainkai 1, Tel: 0931/16777). The roof terrace of Wöhrl Department Store offers another spectacular view (kiosk open in good weather).*

twelve larger-than-life saints. From here, there is a fantastic view of the river, the numerous **church steeples,** the renowned **"Am Stein" vineyards** to the north, the **Marienberg Fortress** rising above the Old Main quarter and the Käppele **Pilgrimage Church** to the south. The first stone bridge across a ford in the river was erected in 1133. Over the centuries, flooding, freezing and even departing German troops in WWII left the bridge in a state of disrepair time and again.

Gates adorned both ends of the bridge in the Middle Ages; hous-

Above: To the left of Marienberg Fortress, the Käppele Pilgrimage Church stands out in the morning sun.

Right: Burkard, Würzburg's first bishop, is represented on the Old Main Bridge.

Town Hall ❹
Beim Grafeneckart 1

Guided tours: May – Oct: Sat 11
Tel: 0931/372609
Meeting point: Town Hall courtyard
across from the fountain
Free

*Above: The Town Hall and Vierröhren Foun-
tain crowned by a statue of Franconia.*

*Above right: The stately Rückermainhof
building in the Karmelitenstrasse behind
the Town Hall.*

*Right: Wenceslas Hall in the Town Hall dates
back to the 13th century.*

The **Grafeneckart** is the oldest portion of the **Town Hall** complex and
the sole remaining Romanesque
secular building in Würzburg. The
tower and the lower side stories
were built as the seat of the bishop's burgrave **Eckart** in 1200. **Wenceslas Hall** is located in a side tract
of the building and is almost as old.
In 1316 the town council purchased
the building and found themselves
the owners of a well-situated town
hall. Additional stories were added
to the tower in the 15th century as
well as the first public **clock.** The
painted **Green Tree** symbolizes the

court of lay assessors that used to meet here under a tree. Further expansions to the structure followed. During the turbulent years of strife between the bishop's princes, the burghers made use of the Town Hall to demonstrate their desire for political independence. The so-called **Red Building** on the left was constructed in 1659/60 in the late Renaissance style and in the 19th century, the Town Hall was expanded to the north to include the former **Carmelite White Friar Monastery**.

TIP: *A room on the ground floor in memory of March 16, 1945, is open daily. It features an accurate model of the extensive damage.*

Vierröhren Fountain ❼

Lucas van der Auvera and **Peter Wagner** designed this Baroque fountain in 1766. Four allegorical female figures embody the cardinal virtues of wisdom, justice, bravery and moderation. Franconia, the patron saint of **Franconia**, crowns the obelisk. The fountain was supplied with fresh water from outside

the town as early as 1733. This fountain has always served as a popular meeting point and one special tradition was washing out empty change purses early Shrove Tuesday morning. Rumor had it that the purse would be filled all the sooner after the washing.

TIP: *The night watchman begins his colorful tale and tour of the city here (See Practical Info section).*

Halfway down the Domstrasse is **Sternplatz Square** with its delight-

constructed apartment house and shop is located at the south end of the Market Place (House Nr. 14/16). The building was to mark the beginning of a beautification project. Its floor plan was extremely functional: seven stores, each with its own storage area and cellar, surround a courtyard. Two floors of apartments above the ground floor provided living quarters for the shop owners. Next door on House Nr. 12 is a plaque commemorating the birthplace of the sculptress **Emy Roeder** (see Granary Museum).

Mary's Chapel ❸
Marienplatz 2

The late Gothic Mary's Chapel immediately catches the eye although its history is nothing to be proud of. This was the **Jewish quarter** in the late Middle Ages and by 1349, it was burned to the ground and its inhabitants murdered. Later the area was turned into a Market Place and in place of a synagogue, a wooden chapel was erected. Bishop **Gerhard von Schwarzenburg** laid the foundation stone for a new church to be built in stone. The burghers financed the nave in the mid 15th century and took charge of further construction in order to demonstrate their self-assuredness and a clear line between the townspeople and the prince-bishop's power. No costs were spared: **flying buttresses** featuring Neumann's statues of Christ, the apostles and John the Baptist adorn the exterior walls. **Tilman Rie-**

ful modern fountain. Take a short detour down the Sterngasse to **Franziskanergasse** where two famous inhabitants once resided. **Tilman Riemenschneider** lived at House Nr.1. The remains of his home and workshop are easy to discern in the newer construction. Later**, Balthasar Neumann** resided across the street at House Nr. 2. The postwar reconstruction added the famous **"Neumann pulpit"** to the roof. From this roof terrace Neumann could observe the progress of various construction sites without leaving home.

The Market Place

The Market Place is north of the Domstrasse and features **Andreas Gärtner's obelisk** from 1805. It is appropriately decorated with female statues representing the four seasons. **Balthasar Neumann's** re-

Above: Tilman Riemenschneider's statues of Adam and Eve adorn the south entrance of Mary's Chapel.
Right: A statue of the Virgin Mary appropriately crowns the spire of the church dedicated to her.

menschneider's portrayal of **Adam** and **Eve** from 1493 flank the south portal. The city councilors were so pleased with Riemenschneider's statues that they gave him a bonus (originals in the Main-Franconian Museum in the Fortress).

The tympanum above the north portal depicts the **Annunciation** with the Baby Jesus sliding down a type of speaking tube into the Virgin's ear.

Inside a plaque on one of the columns in the nave commemorates the architect, **Balthasar Neumann,** who is buried in this chapel. Several effigies line the walls; of special note is **Konrad von Schaumberg's** designed by **Tilman Riemenschneider** in 1502 on the west wall. In 1582 the goldsmith **Johannes Kilian** created the silver **Madonna.** The tiny

Above: High walls in the Gothic sanctuary of Mary's Chapel.

Right: Hustle and bustle at the Market Place in front of the House to the Falcon.

shops snuggled on the outer walls of the church are part and parcel of this house of worship; the first ones were rented out in 1437.

House to the Falcon ❷
Marktplatz 9

The House to the Falcon on the upper Market Place started out life as a pub. In 1751 the innkeeper's widow Meissner commissioned traveling Upper Bavarian craftsmen to carry out the delightful Rococo stuccowork on the façade. A falcon on the roof was added to the building at the same time. This sumptuous decoration certainly attracted customers but more importantly, it was worthy of a tax exemption. An ordinance inspired by Balthasar Neumann stated that owners of especially attractive façades received a tax rebate.

Nowadays the **Tourist Office** and **Ticket Service** are housed in this gem. For example, tickets for the Mozart Festival are on sale here prior to and during the concert season.

> **TIP:** *The Public Library has also found a home within these splendid walls. The Readers' Café has a wide assortment of dailies and the Internet Café offers Internet access for a small fee.*

Gressengasse

A charming dark red and beige corner building with an oriel and voluted gables stands out on the west side of the Market Place. This lovingly refurbished structure from 1590 currently houses the Castell Bank. The **Stachel Wine Inn** ❾ is located a few steps further along the Gressengasse. A 17th century inner courtyard embellished with balustrades and lush green foliage reveals itself behind the 12th century double portal. It was in this pub during the **Peasants' War** that rebellious peas-

ants are said to have met with **Florian Geyer** to negotiate a strategy against the bishop. Most likely, the wine inn derived its name from this period; Stachel translates into **morning star**, a medieval cutting weapon.

> **TIP:** *A visit to this idyllic courtyard for a light meal or dinner accompanied by a glass of Franconian wine is an unforgettable experience. ("Zum Stachel" Wine Inn, Gressengasse 1, Tel: 0931/52770).*

The Marktgasse leads to the Karmelitengasse and the stately **Rückermainhof** (Karmelitenstrasse 20) with its ornate red sandstone façade. **Joseph Greising** was the architect of this early 18th century edifice that originally served as a district office for the St. Burkard knightly charitable institution.

The **Fish Market** was held on the small square on the other side of the street and thus closer to the river. Fish fresh from the Main River was a stable for years on end. In the oldest guidebook on Würzburg, the author, Carl Gottfried Scharold, listed almost two dozen types of fish and crayfish that were caught

in the river. The 18th century **Fisher-man's Fountain** is a reminder of this former busy market. Kärrnergasse runs parallel to Karmelitengasse and is connected by passageways. This is where the carters lived; men who used their wooden carts to transport goods from the river to individual houses. A wall painting above a simple entryway to the river quay is all that remains of the original wooden portal. The harbor has long since disappeared as well as the waves from the water mill that tempted daring boys to jump in. Instead, there is an oasis of green

here that is popular due to its proximity to the river and the view of the Marienberg. Young and old alike gather here on warm summer nights and a **beer garden** under the trees for the thirsty is not far off on the bastion of the Old Crane.

Old Crane ⑧
Kranenkai 1

Balthasar Neumann's son, **Franz Ignaz**, constructed this technical marvel in 1773. The crane was used to load and unload the ships in port. The muscle strength of two men in a double wooden tread wheel was needed to start the mechanism. The Old Crane was incorporated into the Baroque fortifications protecting the riverfront. This marked the end of the city walls that continued down the Juliuspromenade in the Middle Ages.

For hundreds of years, Würzburg thrived from its location on the Main River. Fishermen and shipbuilders

Above: It was in the Stachel Wine Inn that the peasants met to negotiate during the Peasants' War.

Left: Decorative balustrades offer a charming backdrop to Stachel's inner courtyard.

in the Main quarter benefitted great-
ly as did the horse-drawn barges
that docked in this old harbor to unload their wares before being pul-
led further upstream. Carters made their living by unloading the building materials and firewood from
the surrounding forests along the
river.

On washdays, the soft river water
attracted Würzburg housewives
and servants well into the 20th century; one of the washing ships from
the 1960s reminiscent of the days
when women were still burdened
by physical household drudgery is
docked near the Old Crane. The river
was definitely part and parcel of
daily life.

Boat Trips
Kranenkai

The white fleet of ships begins its
journey to the town of **Veitshöchheim** near the Old Crane. Tickets
can be purchased at the quay (see
Practical Info).

Juliusspital Charitable Institution ❺
Juliuspromenade 19
Tel.: 0931 / 3 931406

*Above: The Old Crane on a Baroque bas-
tion. Nowadays, pleasure boats dock here.*
*Right: The wooden tread wheel inside the
Old Crane.*

Guided tours in season: Fri 17 (1 hr.),
Sat 17 (1 ½ hrs. + 3 wine samples);
meeting point at the fountain
in the Juliusspital gardens
www.juliusspital.de

A sandstone relief above the **portal** to the Juliuspromenade portrays the laying of the cornerstone by Prince-bishop **Julius Echter** in 1576. This charitable institution built at the edge of town was to serve "the poor and the frail, the old, the sick and the abandoned". In order to have room enough for the large complex, Echter had the **Jewish cemetery** leveled. After a fire in 1699, Antonio Petrini and **Joseph Greising** designed a statelier north wing (Fürstenbau). The **Four Rivers Fountain** in the gardens Is from the same period. **Jacob van der Auvera** created the reclining figures that represent Franconia's rivers. The gold and white **Garden Pavilion** is adjacent. It is difficult to conceive that this lovely building served as a "theatrum anatomicum" or lecture hall for anatomy in the 18th and 19th centuries.

TIP: *The Rococo Apothecary with its original furnishings in the Juliusspital Charitable Institution is a must.*
Mon – Fri 14 – 15 (entrance from the courtyard; please ring bell).
Tel: 0931/393-2311

Vineyards formed the economic basis of this charitable institution from the very beginning. The vast **wine cellars** under the hospital are still in use. The wooden barrel cellar in the **Petrini** wing alone is 250 meters in length. The Juliusspital, one of the three largest wineries in Franconia and one of the largest in Germany, owns prestigious vineyards in Würzburg and Franconia. Its wine fests

take on the form of cultural fests with temporary exhibits and musical programs. **Wine tasting** is best done in the Juliusspital Wine Inn (Weinstube Juliusspital, Juliuspromenade 19, Tel: 0931/54080).

Wine Purchase:
Weineck Julius Echter

Above: The elegant Baroque Garden Pavilion.
Above right: The unique Rococo Apothecary in the Juliusspital Hospital.
Center: The Four Rivers Fountain is a fitting enhancement to the gardens of the Juliusspital.

Koellikerstrasse ½
Tel: 0931/3931450
Mon – Fri 9 – 18, Sat 9 – 16

The Four Rivers Fountain

Jakob van der Auvera, having just arrived from the Flemish town of Mecheln, was commissioned to create the pompous Baroque fountain for the Juliusspital Gardens between 1706 and 1708. The statues represent the four major rivers in Franconia: the Main, the Saale, the Sinn and the Tauber. The mythical griffin, the heraldic symbol of Prince-bishop **Johann Philipp von Greiffenclau**, rises above the nymphs and river god with his urn and above the wa-

ter splashing out of the mouths of fish. This prince-bishop should not be confused with a later Greiffenclau, Carl Philipp, one of the builders of the Residence.

St. Augustine's
Dominikanerplatz 2

Originally this was a **Dominican monastery.** The early Gothic **choir** of the church was consecrated in 1279 and in the 18th century **Balthasar Neumann** came up with plans for a new nave. **Antonio Bossi** carried out the stuccowork in the old choir. In 1813 the **Augustine order** moved into the empty Dominican monastery because they had been forced to vacate their own monastery upon secularization in 1804. Much of the church was badly damaged in World War II. Nikolaus Treu's 1771 **"Sea Victory over the Turks"** depicting the Christian fleet at Lepanto on the High Altar survived. This victory is immortalized in the Dominican rosary prayer.

Stift Haug Church ⑥
Corner of Bahnhofstrasse/ Heinestrasse

This canon-run charitable institution was first located on a rise where the train station is nowadays. When new, wider walls were erected around the town after the Thirty Years' War, the institution was forced to move. Its current location was an excellent tradeoff. The church was constructed by the South Tyrolean architect, **Antonio Petrini**, who came to Würzburg in 1660. His imposing dome is often compared to that of the Cathedral's. His contemporaries considered his plans so uncanny that rumors spread that the devil himself had had a hand in the construction. The original furnishings and décor in the interior have disappeared over time but there is an impressive crucifixion painting by **Jacopo Tintoretto** hanging on loan from Munich in the choir.

Bürgerspital to the Holy Ghost
Semmelstrasse 2

Seasonal guided tours: Sat 14; tickets in wine shop
Monthly wine tasting
Tel: 0931/3503451
Glockenspiel daily at 11, 13, 15, 17
www.buergerspital.de

This charitable institution was first known as the "new" **charitable institution** when it was founded in 1316 and nowadays it is renowned as the oldest charitable institu-

Left: Magnificent stuccowork is on display in the interior of St. Augustine's.
Right: The wine cellars in the Bürgerspital to the Holy Ghost.

tion for burghers in the city. The small Gothic **church** dates back to the institution's beginnings and it is the final resting place of the founders, Johannes and Mergardis von Steren. The south wing on the street side was reconstructed after WWII. Andreas Müller's most pleasing courtyard with red and ochre bands of sandstone still manages to offer peace and quiet as in the old days.

Here too, wine has played a significant role over the centuries. Various donations have made it the third largest winery in Franconia and like the Juliusspital, it too has prestigious appellations such as Abtsleite, Stein and Stein-Harfe.

The Bürgerspital holds two different **wine fests**: one in the courtyard every summer and one at the winery near the Pfaffenberg appellation.

Typically Franconian fare is served in the wine pub (Theaterstrasse 19, Tel: 0931/35288-0) and in the **wine shop** (Ludwigstrasse 1a, Tel: 0931/3503-456).

Wine Purchase
On the corner beneath the glockenspiel
Tel: 0931/3503-403
Mon – Fri 9 – 18, Sat 9 – 15

St. Johannis' Church
Rennweger Ring 1
This Protestant parish church behind the Residence is similar in concept to the Gedächtniskirche or Memorial Church in Berlin. Reinhard Riemerschmied incorporated the tower ruins of the previous neo-Gothic church into his postwar construction.

High above the City – the Marienberg Fortress

Celtic princely residence – walled fortifications and an extensive view – a 100-meter deep well inside a decorative temple – Riemenschneider Collection – bastions and casemates – Neumann's Machicolation Tower – two museums and a princely garden

Left: Marienberg Fortress crowns the steep slope above the Old Main quarter.
Above: Kilian's Tower at the entrance to the second courtyard.

A Mighty Fortress

This is where the prince-bishops literally walled themselves in: walls and bastions surrounding the central fortress that became technically more sophisticated and far more extensive over time. By the 19th century, however, military fortification had reached its limits and nowadays, the Marienberg remains a fascinating fortified complex that houses two important museums: the Main-Franconian Museum and the Prince's Apartments.

Marienberg Fortress

Oberer Burgweg
Tel.: 0931 / 355170

Fortifications open daily: free
Museum shop in the passage to second courtyard
Guided tours (Mary's Chapel, Well House, casemates & Princely Garden): mid-March to end of Oct:
Tues – Fri 11, 14, 15, 16
Sat, Sun & holidays also at 10 & 13
Tickets in Museum Shop; combination ticket includes Princely Apts.
www.schloesser.bayern.de

History

The steep hill rising from the river was always an optimal place for a fortified settlement. Excavations have revealed Greek ceramic shards belonging to powerful Celtic princes who resided here in the **Hallstattian period**. It is likely that **Main-Franconian dukes** had a castle here in the 8th century. Immina, the daughter of the last duke, turned the castle over to **Burkard**, the bishop of Würz-

Don't miss

1. Riemenschneider Collection, Main-Franconian Museum
2. Mary's Church
3. Well House and deep well
4. Princely Garden
5. Medieval model of Würzburg, Fürstenbau Museum
6. Bronze ritual wagon, Main-Franconian Museum
7. Machicolation Tower

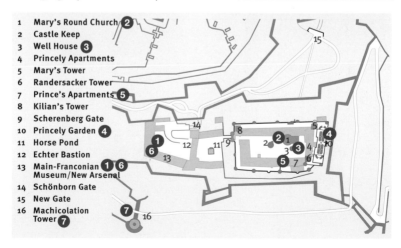

1. Mary's Round Church
2. Castle Keep
3. Well House
4. Princely Apartments
5. Mary's Tower
6. Randersacker Tower
7. Prince's Apartments
8. Kilian's Tower
9. Scherenberg Gate
10. Princely Garden
11. Horse Pond
12. Echter Bastion
13. Main-Franconian Museum/New Arsenal
14. Schönborn Gate
15. New Gate
16. Machicolation Tower

burg, in exchange for the Karlburg Convent. This exchange later became a contentious issue between the townspeople and the bishop because the burghers felt that the bishop's holdings were an unfair advantage. Bishop **Konrad** began construction on a fortress in 1200 and several decades later, his suc-

Above: Scherenberg Gate above the ditch prevented the enemy entry into the inner courtyard.

cessors made the Marienberg their permanent residence. During the Peasants' War in 1525, the revolting peasants backed by the townspeople besieged the fortress but failed to take it. This gave Prince-bishop **Konrad von Thüngen** enough time to call in outside troops, which resulted in a devastating defeat for the peasants. During the **Thirty Years' War**, the Swedish Army did take the fortress and as a result, fortifications in both the town and on the

hill were expanded and improved making a longer enemy siege unlikely. Although the Baroque bastions in the city itself have disappeared, they still are intact at the Marienberg and in the city quarter underneath the fortress.

Visiting the Marienberg

Start at the **Princely Garden** ❹ and enjoy the view of the city and river valley (entry through the Burghof courtyard). Next visit the inner Burghof and **Mary's Church** ❷, the **Well House** ❸ and castle keep. Here is also the entry to the **Princely Apartments** ❺ located in the wing facing the city. Retrace your steps through Scherenberg and Echter gates to the first courtyard to the **Main-Franconian Museum** which houses the magnificent **Riemenschneider Collection** ❶. Com-

Above: The New Gate, completed in 1648, bears the coat-of-arms of Prince-bishop Johann Philipp von Schönborn.

Right: Medieval round watchtowers kept the enemy at bay.

plete your tour with a walk along the paths around the fortifications (entry to Greiffenclauhof left of the Echter bastion).

The struggle for power between the burghers and the bishop having ended plus the fact that the prince-bishops desired a more representative place to dwell, led to the construction of the **Residence** in the city in the 18th century. The Marienberg lost its significance as a princely residence but maintained its military importance during the **French Revolutionary** and **Napoleonic Wars** (1792-1815). During the **Austro-Prussian War** in 1866 when the Prussians were positioned near the Käppele on Nikolausberg Hill and had a direct shot at the Marienberg, they immediately set fire to one of the buildings. Fortunately, the very next day a general ceasefire was called which put an end to the firing. The lesson learned was that the Marienberg fortifications were no longer capable of withstanding modern heavy artillery. In 1867 the Bavarian government officially declared the castle no longer fortified.

The Fortifications

Construction of the fortifications began in the 13th century on the east

side above the steep slope rising from the river. A deep ditch offered protection in the west. The buildings around the inner courtyard are no longer original. Fires burned out whole sections of the complex and prince-bishops refurbished time and again. The sole reminder of the early fortress is the unadorned **castle keep** whose ground floor served as a dungeon and therefore is inaccessible from the courtyard.

It is assumed that a church was already here in the 8th century. Whether or not it actually was **Mary's Church ❷** is unclear. Many an expert are of the opinion that the current structure wasn't erected until the early 11th century. A

choir was added to the east of the church around 1600 and around the same time, **Michael Kern** designed the decorative, ornate portal. **Effigies** of 21 bishops are embedded in the floor of the sanctuary and a centuries-old custom permitted only the entrails of these holy men to be buried here.

The **well** is also medieval; the rockshaft was dug 100 meters down to reach two sources. A stone con-

Above: The inner courtyard with Mary's Round Church, the castle keep and the Well House.

Right: Nowadays, ornate altars grace the niches in Mary's Church.

struction hid the festive octagonal Renaissance **Well House** ❸ during the Thirty Years' War in order to prevent this essential water supply from being fired upon. Renovations in the 1930s unveiled the temple-like structure for the first time in almost 300 years. The Well House was completely restored and a golden statue of **Fortuna** carried out by a local, Fried Heuler, once again crowned the structure.

Three watchtowers guard the inner courtyard. **Kilian's Tower** to the north is from the initial building phase while the burghers were forced to erect **Randersacker Tower** to the southeast in 1308 as punishment for an unsuccessful riot. **Tilman Riemenschneider** was held prisoner here after the peasants were defeated in 1525. The most recent addition, **Mary's Tower** with its gilded Madonna with a halo, serves purely aesthetic purposes.

Bishop **Rudolf von Scherenberg** whose effigy by **Riemenschneider** is in the Cathedral had the western gate bearing his name rebuilt

and decorated with a statue of the **Virgin** in a niche at the top and **Kilian, Totnan** and **Kolonat** below. Scherenberg's successor, **Lorenz von Bibra**, had the princely apartments facing the city refurbished in a statelier manner. The so-called **Bibra spiral stairway** leading up to its own tower on the courtyard side of the complex is also his doing. The first courtyard with a **horse pond** west of the inner courtyard was under the rule of **Julius Echter**. Echter had already had a **library**

and winter apartment built in the south wing but both burned to the ground. Another fire caused him to have to rebuild a major portion of the north wing as well.

Princely Garden ❹

Apr – Oct: 9 - 17:30

A small terrace on the town side of the fortress was turned into a princely garden in the 17th century. Geometric flowerbeds, fountains and statues were later Baroque ad-

ditions. Its unusual position and unique shape are said to resemble a ship or gondola.

Julius Echter von Mespelbrunn
(1545-1617)

*The significant role that this prince-bishop played is made evident by the fact that his **coat-of-arms,** three diagonal rings, can still be found in numerous towns. The second of nine children, he grew up in **Mespelbrunn Castle** in the Spessart Forest. He studied in Leuven, Paris and Rome and then was admitted to the Cathedral Chapter. A short time later in 1573, he was elected **prince-bishop**. He immediately took over the administration and instituted a policy of reforms. His legacy includes the founding of the **Juliusspital Charitable Organization** (1576) and the **university** (1582).The leitmotif of his rule was the Counter-Reformation and in order to strengthen the Catholic faith, he had over 300 churches either refurbished or newly built. These houses of worship all share a similar characteristic: a steep spire whose roof is called an **"Echter bonnet."** Echter drove out the Protestants and instigated regular witch hunts which quickly got out of hand in Würzburg. He died in 1617 on the eve of the Thirty Years' War.*

In 1631 in the midst of the Thirty Years' War, the Swedes overran the Echter bastion west of the horse pond despite its thick side bastions. The troops lay siege to the fortress and plundered everything in sight including the Echter library that eventually became a part of the university in Uppsala.

Left: The Princely Garden offers an excellent view of the city below and the hills beyond.
Above: The sun sets behind Nikolausberg Hill; the towers are those of the Marienberg Fortress.

of which the garrison could bring fire on the dead space at the base of the tower. Neumann designed an indespensible vaulted **passageway** to connect the freestanding four-story tower to the casemates of the bastion. **Jakob van der Auvera** designed the coat-of-arms for Prince-bishop **Christoph Franz von Hutten**, who had commissioned the bulwark.

A further courtyard, Greiffenclau courtyard, was constructed at the end of the 17th century to complement the two westernmost courtyards. The Main-Franconian Museum is located in the buildings in this outermost courtyard.

Main-Franconian Museum
Tel.: 0931 / 20594-0

Apr – Oct: Tues – Sun 10 – 17
Nov – March: Tues – Sun 10 – 16
Audio-guided tour in English (fee)

Combination ticket with Princely Apts.

www.mainfraenkisches-museum.de

Machicolation Tower

Open upon request
Tel: 0931/35517-0
www.schloesser.bayern.de

From 1724-1729, **Balthasar Neumann** oversaw the construction of one of the final defensive towers, Machicolation Tower, which rises above the south flank of the Marienberg on the Innere Leiste slope. Its name is derived from the 21 slots in the platform jutting out from the tower by means

Above: A 14th century clock in the Main-Franconian Museum.

Center: A rare artifact: a Bronze Age ritual wagon.

Right: Riemenschneider's original statues of Adam and Eve created for Mary's Church at the Market Place.

The museum is a true tourist attraction due to its excellent and varied collection of works of art and artifacts from the Main-Franconian region. The **Riemenschneider Hall** ❶ contains the most extensive collection of works by the master craftsman.

The history of the museum dates back to 1913 when it opened in the Maxstrasse near the Residence un-

der the name of Franconian Luitpold Museum. The museum was bombed out in 1945 but just two years later, it reopened at the Marienberg. Ever since, the former **arsenal, military headquarters** and **Echter bastion** have provided 5,400 m² of exhibit space. The museum offers an extremely wide array of treasures; only a few can be highlighted here.

These treasures span the centuries from the Bronze Age through the

Tilman Riemenschneider
(ca. 1460-1531)

The woodcarver and sculptor was born in 1460 in the Thuringian town of Heiligenstadt as the son of a mint master; he grew up in Osterode in the Harz region. After completing an apprenticeship, his journeyman's travels took him to Schwaben and to the Upper Rhine area, along the Moselle River and probably to Holland as well. He settled in Würzburg as an apprentice in 1483 and two years later, he married his master's widow, Anna Schmidt, and in short order, he inherited a house, became a citizen and a recognized master of his trade.

Word of his superb work such as the sculptures of Adam and Eve at Mary's Chapel soon spread and Riemenschneider's number of commissions increased so that he had to enlarge his workshop. His fame also ensured him a series of political positions.

The situation changed during the Peasants' War when Riemenschneider, the former mayor and a member of the city council, joined the side of the revolting peasants. After their defeat, he was locked in a tower in the fortress and most likely, tortured. Research has dispelled the myth that his hands were broken. Nevertheless, some of his assets were confiscated and after his release, he carried out a few restorations but never carved or sculpted again. After his death in 1531, his work was almost completely forgotten. Riemenschneider was one of the most skilled masters of the late Gothic; his faces depict a deep sense of grief and suffering, his figures are delicate, the folds of his robes flow and his expressive hands tell a tale of their own. Numerous examples of his ingenuity and that of his workshop are on display in the Main-Franconian Museum.

19th century. Many **original statues** are on display here for safekeeping whereas copies now stand in their former location.

A special attraction in the Prehistoric and Ancient History Gallery is the 3,000 year old bronze **ritual wagon** ❻ featuring four lively birds' heads on the axis. This model of a larger version was discovered in Acholshausen, a town south of Würzburg. The collection further includes a variety of excavated objects such as jewelry, fibula, coins, chalices, ax-

Above: Tilman Riemenschneider's gravestone was discovered at the Cathedral.

Right: Nikolaus Neeb designed this wrought iron gate that decorates the entrance to the Winepress Hall.

es and hatchets. There are medieval vessels such as the decorated glass beakers from a wealthy burgher family in Würzburg. Whoever is interested in Franconian traditional costumes, daily utensils, rustic farm furniture and folk art should visit the **Folk Art Gallery.**

In addition to the exquisite porcelain, glass, faience and furniture in **Baroque and Rococo Gallery, Ferdinand Tietz's** original frolicsome stone sculptures designed for the palace gardens in Veitshöchheim are on display. There is also an extensive collection of bozzetti, true-to-scale miniature statues that were used to execute larger-than-life statues.

The **Art Gallery** contains paintings and sketches and viticulture is on display in the **Winepress Hall.**

Prince's Apartments or Fürstenbaumuseum
Including the History of Würzburg Gallery
Tel.: 0931 / 355170

End of March to Oct: Tues – Sat 9 – 18
www.schloesser.bayern.de
www.mainfraenkisches-museum.de

The **Prince's Apartments** facing the city still bear witness to the medieval palace. Restoration work after WWII was ongoing until 1990 when the museum was opened. The galleries as well as the architecture are noteworthy. The apartments display furniture, tapestries and paintings; on display are the Bibra apartment as well as the Prince's Hall with early Gothic arcades and Julius Echter's family tree. There is also a **Treasury** containing Communion vessels and liturgical vestments.

The second floor retells the history of the city of Würzburg from the 8th

to the 20th century. A **model** of the city ❺ depicts Würzburg in 1525 towards the end of the Middle Ages.

Getting to the Fortress

Travel by **car** is via Höchberger-strasse and Oberer Burgweg. Ample parking for a fee.

Bus 9 leaves from the Residence via the Juliuspromenade and Kulturspeicher Museum to the Marienberg (Apr – Nov 1). **Bus 18** goes year round to the Oberer Burgweg bus stop around 500 meters from the entrance.

A charming **walk** starts at the Old Main Bridge across the Zellerstrasse and Tellsteige to the Fortress (elevation gain c. 100 meters).

A longer path starts behind St. Burkard's Church in the Old Main quarter and zigzags through vineyards and passes the **Machicolation Tower** on the south slope and enters the fortifications from the west. Yet another path starts at the Friedensbrücke Bridge (corner Luitpold/Dreikönigsstrasse) and passes through garden scenery and fortified walls but offers no wide views.

Walking up to the Marienberg Fortress is definitely preferable to taking the bus or driving since the paths are varied and allow the rambler to get a feel for what the enemy with all his armor and weaponry had to accomplish in order to lay siege to the castle. The climb is gentle and there are benches along the way.

Right: The lines of fortification resemble the lines of growth on a tree trunk; Machicolation Tower is clearly visible in the foreground.

Käppele Pilgrimage Church and the Old Main quarter –

Neumann's Käppele Pilgrimage Church – 256 steps and Mary's footprint – the oldest quarter and the oldest church in the city – where Leonard Frank's THE BAND OF ROBBERS grew up

Left: A winter walk past one of the Stations of the Cross below the Käppele.
Above: St. Burkard's in the Old Main quarter.

From the Tradesmen's Quarter to the Pilgrimage Church

The Old Main quarter is the oldest part of the city and although it is just a narrow strip between the Main River and the Marienberg, it boasts a surprising number of sights including the impressive Burkard Gate. In the good old days when a local passed through this gate to climb to the Käppele on Nikolausberg Hill, he was leaving the city on an excursion. The gate was locked every night.

Visiting the Quarter

Begin at the far side of the **Old Main Bridge** at the **Spitäle ❺**. Walk right to **Deutschhaus Church ❸**. Return to the Spitäle and walk through Burkarderstrasse towards **St. Burkard's Church**. Make a detour into the right narrow lane that is packed with small houses (Spitalgasse 1, 2, 3 and Felsengasse) reminiscent of the past. Visit **St. Burkard's ❷** and then take the path that leads under the choir to the former **prison for women ❹** and on to **Burkard Gate ❻**. The path leading up to **Käppele ❶** starts here and continues straight to Leistenstrasse; cross it to Mergentheimerstrasse and go right into Nikolausstrasse. After a few meters, a path on the left leading up to the **Stations of the Cross** and the Käppele comes into view.

Don't miss
❶ *Käppele and Stations of the Cross*
❷ *St. Burkard's Church*
❸ *Deutschhaus Church*
❹ *Former Prison for Women*
❺ *Spitäle*
❻ *Burkard Gate*

The Käppele can also be reached by car or bus (see Practical Info).

Excursion

In the 19th century the Beautification Association began to plant the barren heights in and around Würzburg, the outcome of which is still appreciated. The **Frankenwarte** recreation area on Nikolausberg behind the Käppele was a part of this project. Access is by car or bus 35. In conjunction with the **Steinbachtal Valley** nearby, miles of paths are just a short distance from the city. The historical **Frankenwarte Tower**

at the top of the plateau offers extensive 360° views on clear days (turnstile fee).

A good view of the Main River valley can be enjoyed from the Nikolaushof Restaurant (outdoor seating), Johannisweg, Tel: 0931/79750-0 or Schützenhof Restaurant, Mainleitenweg 48, Tel: 0931/72422.

Old Main Quarter

The area surrounding the Marienberg Fortress was settled early on, most likely there was some sort of fortification here already in the 7th century since this compact space between the hill and the river was easy to fortify. Bishop **Burkard** founded the first church in the city here along with **St. Andreas Monastery** that has long since disappeared. As the city grew, this narrow strip left little room for development especially after the focal point of the city was repositioned to

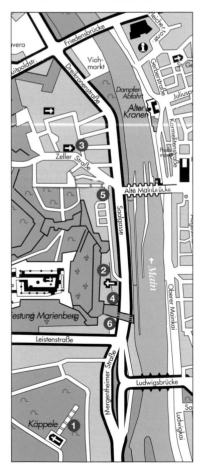

Left: View from the bastion past the Burkard Gate and the former Prison for Women.

Above: Frankenwarte Tower stands at the highest point in the city's environs.

the Cathedral quarter. This **Old Main quarter** became the home of fishermen and tradesmen and the steep, narrow streets still contain some of the flair of bygone days.

Burkard Gate ❻ *and the Former Prison for Women* ❹

Passing under St. Burkard's choir to the south, the traveler comes upon a small square with a building erected in 1810 that has a rather severe façade. This was originally a **prison for women** and the unusual façade bears admonishing signs and symbols. The ten columns, for example, represent the Ten Commandments. **Peter Speth** designed the Classical structure influenced by the architecture of the French Revolution. No longer a prison, it is currently home to the Cairo Youth Center.

Burkard Gate is on the south side of the square and in 1680 it was constructed as a part of **Antonio Petrini's** new Baroque city fortifications. Its long winding entryway kept enemy fire at bay and nowadays this passageway is reserved for pedestrians and cyclists.

St. Burkard's ❷

Burkarderstrasse 42

The church has a turbulent history. In 750 **Burkard,** the first bishop of Würzburg, founded **St. Andreas**

Monastery which doubled as his bishopric. The monastery was deprived of this function with the construction of the Cathedral on the other side of the river. After a fire in the 11th century, the church had to be rebuilt. At the end of the 15th century, a new **choir** and **transept** were added and in the 17th century, the west end had to be torn down in order to make room for a navigational canal and a water supply to a mill between the church and the hillside. As compensation, the choir was finally completed but it had to be elevated in order to allow a street to pass under it. The various building phases are easy to identify in the interior. The church's most valuable treasure has to be a bust of the **Virgin**, an early work by **Tilman Riemenschneider.** In the narthex on the way to the vineyards is a **Mount of**

Left: The Romanesque nave of St. Burkard's had to be shortened in order to make room for a canal.
Above: Baroque altars adorn the transept in St. Burkard's.

Olives group sculpted by **Wolfgang van der Auvera**.

> **TIP:** *After passing through the gate by the Mount of Olives, the path of the former canal can be made out. The small lake in front of Burkard Gate was also a part of the canal.*

Walking down Burkarderstrasse leads past **Balthasar Neumann's** first owned home. It is a simple row house (Nr. 28-32) built at the beginning of Neumann's career for himself and two other court administrators.

Spitäle ❺
Zellerstrasse 1
Tel.: 0931 / 44119

Tues – Thurs, Sat, Sun, holidays 11 – 18, Fri 11 – 20
Free
www.vku-kunst.de

The Classical temple **façade** of the former Court Charitable Institution Church greets the traveler from the Old Main Bridge. The Spitäle and a gate arcade are all that remain of the 15th century **Court Charitable Institution to the 14 Auxiliary Saints**. Nowadays, a regional art society holds temporary exhibits in the building.

Deutschhaus Church ❸
Zellerstrasse 36
The Protestant Deutschhaus Church stands out prominently in the north-

ern part of the Old Main quarter. It was erected in 1219 by the **Order of Teutonic Knights** who had settled there. The late Romanesque tower was completed before the actual church; its Baroque **helmet roof** is of a later date. Minimal bomb damage was done to the beautiful Gothic sanctuary in 1945. However, its function as a military storage depot in the 19th century did cause some damage to the interior.

Käppele ❶
Nikolausberg
Tel.: 0931 / 72670 (Capuchin Monastery)

The vernacular name for this **pilgrimage church** on Nikolausberg Hill is Käppele or **small chapel** and it is one of the landmarks of the city. Its origin dates back to the Thirty Years' War when a pilgrimage here to honor the Virgin became more

Above left: The north slopes of the Marienberg Fortress are covered in green.
Left: Lovely Gothic stonework on the south portal of Deutschhaus Church.
Above: Deutschhaus Church high above Zellerstrasse.

and more popular. Its purpose has not wavered over the centuries. In the mid 18th century, the architect, **Balthasar Neumann**, designed this jewel by incorporating the simple pilgrimage chapel there at the time into his total concept. This is one of Neumann's most successful late works that has withstood not only the test of time but also the military attacks on the city. The splendid interior is crowned by **Johann Michael Feichtmayr's** plasterwork in combination with **Matthäus Günther's** ceiling frescos. The central fresco in the dome depicts the crowning of the Virgin and the Virgin as the patron saint of Franconia. The **sanctuary's** glorious Rococo blends

in with the early Classical elements of the pulpit and the High Altar by **Georg Winterstein.** However, in the chapel next door, the stuccowork reminiscent of Materno Bossi's style, is pure Classicism. **Votive offerings** molded in wax and votive pictures line the walls of the **Miracle Corridor** behind the sanctuary. They speak of the fortunes and misfortunes of pious believers.

Above: Neumann's Käppele is one of the city's most prominent landmarks.
Right: The Classical high altar and pulpit are a pleasant contrast to the Käppele's Rococo interior.

It was Balthasar Neumann's drawings that formed the basis for the **Stations of the Cross** on the terraces leading up to the Käppele. **Johann Peter Wagner** designed the statues for the fourteen small chapels that retell the story of the Passion. Plane trees line the 256 steps and legend has it that the Virgin Mary left her **footprint** in stone at the third terrace.

Paths to the Käppele

From Nikolausstrasse climb the **shaded steps** past the Stations of the Cross; **bus 35** leaves from the Sanderring and stops in the Nikolausstrasse before continuing on to the Frankenwarte (Not all buses stop at the bus stop Käppele!).

Travel by **car** up the Nikolausstrasse to the parking lot around 200 meters from the pilgrimage church.

Leonhard Frank
(1882-1961)

*Leonhard Frank grew up in Würzburg in a lower class family. He moved to **Munich** hoping to become an artist, where later instead, he became a writer. His **Band of Robbers** published in 1914 became an instant success. It retells the story of his youth in the Old Main quarter in a nostalgic but also critical manner. Frank, who had moved to Berlin, was considered one of Germany's most renowned authors in the 1920s. His **pacifist views** had already forced him to emigrate during WWI and in 1933, his leftist views were reason enough to flee once again. Strange circumstances led him to emigrate to **America** where he lived until 1950. He spent his remaining years in **Munich**. A memorial **plaque** created by Renate Jung hangs near the Deutschhaus Church.*

More Sights and an Outing

*Old and new universities and the
Science Mile –
Kulturspeicher or Granary
Museum – Shalom Europa –
Siebold, researcher of Japanese
culture – summer palace
and gardens in Veitshöchheim*

Left: View from the Steinberg vineyards of the river and the
Old Main Bridge and Lion's Bridge; the former Customs
House dominates the foreground.
Above: A statue of Prometheus at the New University.

The University, Museums and a Day Trip

Some of the sights described in this chapter are located in the downtown area or border it. The Old University is one such example and the Kulturspeicher or Granary Museum is another. Further museums such as Siebold Museum are hard to reach on foot but are worth a visit. A boat trip to the summer palace in Veitshöchheim is a scenic adventure in itself.

Ring Park

A stroll around this **green belt** that forms a half circle around the town is actually a walk through the **ditch** and **earthworks** in front of the former town fortifications. This area ensured that there was no dead space in front of the walls. The fortifications on the town side of the river were leveled very quickly after the town purchased them in 1868. But then the real debate began as to what this newly-created space should be used as: a building site, a road or a park? The decision was reached in 1880 when the well-known Swedish landscape gardener, **Jens Person Lindahl**, was commissioned to create a park in-

Don't miss

❶ *Granary Museum*

❷ *Old University*

❸ *Röntgen Memorial*

❹ *Shalom Europa Museum*

❺ *Siebold Museum*

A "Must See":

Summer Palace and Rococo Gardens in Veitshöchheim

Above: The steeples and spires that dot the skyline are a reminder of the role the Catholic Church played in Würzburg.

cluding small rises, lawns and lakes as well as flowerbeds and shady trees. Most of his plans were carried through and are still evident. Unfortunately, few townspeople praised his work; in fact he had a very difficult time reaching his objectives and he took his own life in 1887 as a result. A **memorial** to this ill-fated landscape artist is in the park near the Sanderring.

Nowadays the Ring Park serves as a green belt for relaxation near the downtown area. **Klein-Nizza** behind the Residence is a popular spot with

its giant playground, bird aviary and duck ponds. The Ring Park Fest is held every August and offers live music and children's recreational programs.

The Science Mile

In the second half of the 19th century, the sciences and medicine experienced a heyday in Würzburg. Professors of medicine such as **Rudolf Virchow** or **Albert von Kölliker** carried out research and taught at the university here. **Lecture halls** and **labs** soon became overcrowded

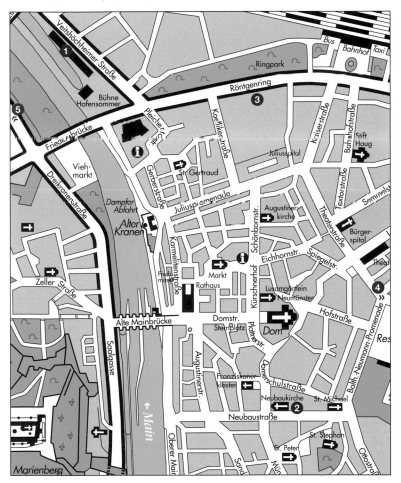

but fortunately this was at the same time that the fortifications were torn down creating new space in the heart of the town. The university was able to build several new stately halls in a short period of time, many still stand today. The Old Eye Clinic, Old Chemistry Hall, the Old Zoological Institute, the Anatomy Hall as well as the Physiology and Old Physics Halls were erected in short order. And the sciences continued to flourish. Of the **thirteen Nobel Prize winners** that until now have worked at the university in Würzburg, ten carried out research in this group of university halls.

Wilhelm Conrad Röntgen
(1845-1923)

The son of a cloth maker was born in Remschied-Lennep. He completed his studies as a mechanical engineer in Switzerland in 1868 and went on to earn his doctorate degree. After carrying out research in Würzburg, Strasbourg, Hohenheim and Giessen, he returned to Würzburg as a full professor of physics in 1888. He discovered the x-ray on the evening of November 8, 1895, and published his findings the following month. He lectured to the Physiological-Medical Society on this remarkable subject in January 1896. In 1900 he took on a full professorship in Munich where he continued his work. The Swedish Academy of Sciences awarded him the first Nobel Prize for Physics in 1901.

TIP: *A walking path with more information on the Nobel Prize winners is across the street in the Ring Park.*

Röntgen Memorial ❸
Röntgenring 8
Tel.: 0931 / 3511-102

Mon – Thurs 8 – 16, Fri 8 – 15
www.wilhelmconradroentgen.de

Wilhelm Conrad Röntgen is the most famous Nobel Prize winner from Würzburg. He discovered the **x-ray** in 1895 in the Old Physiological Institute. His original lab and equipment as well as the **historical lecture hall** are open to the public.

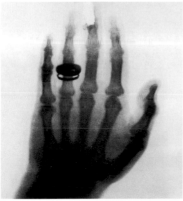

The Pleich Quarter

Although this quarter of town was included in the town walls in the Middle Ages, it nonetheless has retained its village like character. The oldest patrician house in Würzburg, a **craftsman's home** (Pleicherkirchgasse 16) dating back to 1521, is located here. **St. Gertraud's Church** is the focal point of the narrow lanes and squares. This simple hall church was built under Julius Echter's rule in the early 17th century.

Kulturspeicher
or Granary Museum ❶
Veitshöchheimerstrasse 5
Tel.: 0931 / 32225-0

> Tues 13 – 18, Wed, Fri – Sun 11 – 18, Thurs 11 – 19
> Tours accompanying specific exhibits and museum courses
> **www.kulturspeicher.de**

With the help of modern architecture, the **old customs house** at the harbor has been transformed into a 3,500 m² art gallery that opened its doors in 2001. The **City Gallery** has found a new home in the right wing and it concentrates on works by

Left: One of the historical university institutes on the Röntgenring.
Above: Wilhelm Conrad Röntgen's laboratory.
Center: The x-ray of Professor Albert von Koelliker's hand on January 23, 1896.

Main-Franconian artists. The sculptures of **Emy Roeder**, a native of Würzburg, are just one of the highlights. Her Expressionist statue of a pregnant woman is unique. A completely different type of artwork awaits the museumgoer in the other wing where the **Peter C. Ruppert Art Collection** is on display with its 250 paintings, moving works of art and lights in art. This is **Conceptual Art** after 1945. Well-known artists of this genre include Max Bill and Victor Vasarely.

A variety of temporary exhibits accompanies the permanent collections.

The Cultural Mile

Further cultural establishments are located in the Granary Museum complex or within walking distance. Within the complex is the **BBK Gallery**, which features local artists; the tanzSpeicher, which performs contemporary theater; and the **Bockshorn Cabaret Theater.** "Arte Noah" anchored at the harbor is a ship that is oriented towards contemporary art and every summer the **Old Harbor** is the perfect backdrop for the **open air productions.**
(See Practical Info for details)

BKK Gallery
Tel: 0931/50612
Wed – Fri, Sun 11 – 18, Sat 13 – 20

"Arte Noah" Ship
Tel: 0171/ 5454325
Wed – Sat 15 – 18, Sun 13 – 17

TIP: *The museum complex is within walking distance from the Old Crane on the banks of the river*

The Peter's Quarter and the Old University

The area between the Neubaustrasse and Ring Park was, like the Pleich quarter, inside the town fortifications in the Middle Ages.

Old University ❷
Domerschulstrasse 16

The first **university** in Würzburg was founded in 1402 and survived a decade. In contrast, **Julius Echter's university,** built in 1582 is still flourishing. **Georg Robin** designed the four-winged complex that is accessible from the Domerschulstrasse through three stately por-

Left: The Kulturspeicher or Granary Museum is an architectural delight.
Above: A summer evening passes quickly at the harbor behind the Granary Museum.

tals. In 1696, **Antonio Petrini** completed the highest tower at the time in Würzburg, the university church tower, which housed the university observatory. A carillon has long since replaced it. Nowadays, the church serves as a concert hall; the remainder of the complex is used for university purposes and is not open to the public. A closer glance into the lovely courtyard is worth the effort.

To the east is the **priests' seminary,**

Above: The inner courtyard of the Old University with the University Church tower.

Center: Nowadays, the interior of the University Church is used for official ceremonies and concerts.

Right: The New University on Sanderring.

formerly a Jesuit college (Domerschulstrasse 18). The façade was designed by **Joseph Greising**. A plaque on the diocesan archives, a modern building across the street, is dedicated to the **synagogue** which stood behind the structure until 1945.

St. Michael's Church
Josef-Stangl-Platz 1

Philipp Geigel and Michael Fischer designed this early Classical, originally Jesuit, church adjacent to the priests' seminary.

St. Stephan's Church
Wilhelm-Schwinn-Platz

In 1789 Philipp Geigel designed this church that became Protestant in 1803. The postwar reconstruction incorporated the surviving west towers into the modern structure; the 11th century crypt was left undamaged as well.

St. Peter's Church
Petersplatz

The original Romanesque church dates back to the 11th century. In 1717 **Joseph Greising** redesigned the edifice by adding an elegant three-story Baroque façade. The church was almost completely destroyed in WWII but the **Rococo pulpit** by **Wolfgang van der Auvera** managed to survive.

New University
Sanderring 2

This neo-Baroque monumental building was constructed as the "new" university in 1896 and it contains lecture halls and administrative offices. Even newer is the more modern campus from the 1960s at the Hubland.

Carmelite Church
Sanderstrasse 12

This was originally a convent church until 1564; later the Carmelite monks took it over. In 1662 **Antonio Petrini** redesigned the church creating the first Baroque church façade in Würzburg.

Franciscan Monastery and Church
Franziskanergasse 7

www.franziskanerkloster-wuerzburg.de

The Franciscans established their first monastery in Germany in Würzburg in 1221. They moved to the present site in 1249 and soon after, began construction on a church. Its simple Gothic style was reconstructed after 1945. Over a dozen noteworthy **effigies** are housed within the church's walls as well as a **pieta** by **Tilman Riemenschneider** and **Michael Kern's** decorative portal depicting the stigmatization of St. Francis dated 1613. The Gothic **cloister**, an exquisite example of the period, was build between the 13th and the 15th centuries.

Greising Complex
Neubaustrasse 6-12

Four Baroque structures make up this group of **patrician buildings** constructed in the first half of the 18th century under **Balthasar Neumann.** It becomes immediately clear how Neumann intended to redesign the entire town. To the locals, however, this is the Greising Complex.

Further Museums

Shalom Europa ❹
Tel.: 0931 / 404140
Valentin-Becker-Strasse 11
(Busline 6)

Mon – Thurs 10 – 16, Sun 11 – 16
www.shalomeuropa.de

The new **Jewish Museum** and Cultural Center behind the Residence is evidence of a growing Jewish community. The museum not only exhibits Jewish life and traditions in Würzburg, it also has an extensive collection of medieval **tombstones** from the former Jewish cemetery in the Pleich quarter. These historical graves were excavated and preserved in 1987 when a building was torn down.

Jewish Documentation Center
Tel.: 0931 / 373111

Mon – Thurs 13 – 17, Fri 9 – 12
Free
www.wuerzburg.de/stadtarchiv

A permanent exhibition in the cultural center retells the **history of the Jews** in Würzburg.

Siebold-Museum ❺
Frankfurterstrasse 87
Streetcar lines 2 & 4 to Zellerau
Tel.: 0931 / 413541

Tues – Fri 15 – 17, Sat – Sun 10 – 12, 15 – 17
www.wuerzburg.de/siebold-museum

The well-known doctor, researcher and scientist, **Philipp Franz von Siebold**, was born into a scholarly family in Würzburg in 1796. He was one of the first Europeans to research the isolated island of Japan and he wrote numerous ground-

breaking works to acquaint the western world with the Land of the Rising Sun. The museum is located in the villa of a former brewery. Part of the exhibition is dedicated to the influential Siebold family.

Left: The Franciscan Monastery cloister.
Right: The Greising Complex in the Neubaustrasse.
Above: A detail of the exuberant Baroque design of the Greising Complex.

Botanical Gardens
Julius-von-Sachs-Platz 4
Streetcar lines 3 & 5 to Heidingsfeld
Tel.: 0931 / 8886240

Apr – Sept: 8 – 18, Oct – March: 8 – 15:30
Conservatory: Apr – Sept: 8 – 15:30
Free
www.bgw.uni-wuerzburg.de

The university botanical gardens include everything from tropical plants to a vegetable garden. There is also a display of the so-called **Siebold plants** that Philipp Franz von Siebold brought back with him from Japan.

Mineralogical Museum
University at Hubland
Bus 14
Tel.: 0931 / 8885407

Wed 14 – 16, Sun 14 – 17
Free

An interesting collection of precious stones, minerals, crystals and meteorites are on display here.

A Day Trip to Veitshöchheim
St. Veit is one of the auxiliary saints and his remains lie at rest in St. Veit's Cathedral in Prague. He is seated as the beloved symbol of the

town in a three-legged yellow pot on a red shield and has been the patron saint of Veitshöchheim since 1563. St. Veit, in Latin: Vitus; Höchheim translates literally as a settlement on a hill. Towns with "Höchheim" in their names indicate settlements that date back to the middle of the 6th century. Archeological findings have revealed settlements in the area dating back to the Neolithic and Bronze ages.

The **summer palace** and **Rococo Gardens** in Veitshöchheim are renowned. A stroll through the town's narrow streets and past its picturesque historical houses and along the river promenade dotted with outdoor cafes makes for a pleasant outing.

Veitshöchheim, 10 kilometers north of Würzburg, can be reached by car, buses 11 & 19, train, bicycle path or by boat.

Above: High walls surround Oberzell Abbey north of Würzburg.

Right: The town of Veitshöchheim lies behind the summer palace and Rococo Gardens.

TIP: *Boat Trips to Veitshöchheim*
Departure: Kranenkai near the Old Crane
Hourly departures in season
 • *Veitshöchheimer Personenschifffahrt*
Tel: 0931/55633
 • *Schiffstouristik Würzburg*
Tel: 0931/58573

Oberzell Abbey
Zell am Main
Tel.: 0931 / 4601-0

www.oberzell.de

The former abbey peers out above its high walls on the banks of the river. Secularization dissolved the abbey and Koenig & Bauer High Speed Printing Machine Manufacturers found a home here. As the company became a global partner, it moved to larger premises and the complex is currently owned by a socially-active religious group.

Veitshöchheim Summer Palace
Echterstrasse 10, Veitshöchheim
Tel.: 0931 / 91582, 355170

Apr – Oct: Tues – Sun 9 – 18
Guided tours 10 – 12 & 14 – 17 hourly
www.schloesser.bayern.de

This summer palace was originally designed as a **hunting lodge** and **pleasure castle** for the prince-bishops of Würzburg at the end of the 17th century. Prince-bishop **Pe-**

ter **Philipp von Dernbach** commissioned the construction of this retreat. At the end of the 18th century, **Balthasar Neumann** was asked to expand the structure and he turned it into a permanent summer residence. Neumann designed the **staircase** leading to both upper floors as well. Yet he was not the only court architect involved in the improvements. The prince-bishop's summer quarters were located in the southern wing. **Ferdinand von Tuscany,** the successor to the prince-bishops, had the rooms across the hall renovated in the Classical style at the beginning of the 19th century. The rather homey, intimate interior of this palace stands in stark contrast to the stately, representative apartments in the Residence. It is not hard to understand why many a

ruler felt more at home here than in the city.

Rococo Gardens

Open year round; free
Fountain: Apr – end of Oct:
daily 13 – 17 on the hour

The gardens were laid out under Prince-bishop **Adam Friedrich von Seinsheim** between 1763 and 1768. Although the terrain is almost flat,

Above: The charming summer palace in Veitshöchheim.

Center: A cozy pavilion in the Rococo Gardens.

Right: No Rococo garden would be complete without its follies.

the gardens are cleverly landscaped so that they appear very intimate as **Ferdinand Tietz's** amorous statues provide an air of gaiety along the paths and arbors; **Peter Wagner's** figures seem calmer and more refined in the temples and hedged niches. The wooded eastern section is the least gardenlike while the central gardens continue to amaze with their hidden roundels and elegant Rococo benches. The western section is dominated by a large geometrical pond dedicated to poetry. Ferdinand Tietz's statues of Apollo and the muses recline on **Mt. Parnassus** while Pegasus rears at the top.

In the 19th century a new rail line threatened to cut through the middle of the gardens. Fortunately, **Ludwig I** prevented this from happening but a relic from this period is the **train station** directly behind the palace designed in the neo-Renaissance style that had a special waiting room for the ruler.

TIP: *An informative audio guide for the gardens can be obtained at the summer palace.*

Wine and Culture

Franconian wine and joie de vivre –
children's theater, cabaret, music –
performances and calendar of events –
tourist and practical info

Left: Pleasure boats returning from Veitshöchheim dock at the quay near the Old Crane.
Above: Grapes ready for the picking.

Wine and Franconian Love of Life

The very first official written document on Würzburg in **779** mentions **winegrowing** and little has changed since: the Marienberg, the Käppele and the vineyards still characterize the city best. Over the centuries, the culture of wine became a part of daily life expressed in joie de vivre. This is typical for most winegrowing regions. Yet wine was an equally important sector of the economy and Würzburg's main export product. Its popularity was due to the high quality and nature's role in providing the right blend of climate and soil. The **Main River valley** soaks in the rays of sun and provides a buffer for the cold nights. The steep, dry slopes are optimal for capturing the sun's warmth. The grapevines are able to form deep roots in the shell limestone soil and take in the minerals that lend the grapes their distinct taste and aroma. The best known appellations include **Innere Leiste** grown on the south flank of the Marienberg and **Stein wines** grown further to the north. The **Stein-Harfe** appellation forms the heart of these vineyards and derives its name from the harp-shaped location. Even the poet **Goethe** was enamored by Stein wines.

Franconian wines are typically **dry** and in this region, **white.** The most common varieties are **Müller-Thurgau** and **Silvaner** followed by **Riesling, Rieslaner, Kerner, Scheurebe** and **Bacchus.** Red wines such as **Domina** and **Schwarzriesling** have been

growing in popularity. Each of these varieties has it own typical but unique texture. The character and the quality of a wine is a combination of bouquet, terrain, year and how the grapes are grown. Wine connoisseurs speak in terms of fruity, metallic or true to the grape and even if one's vocabulary doesn't include these terms in conjunction with wine, a taste of Franconian wine culture should not be passed up.

Bocksbeutel

This **flat-bellied** bottle has been in use in the region for around 250 years and is a sign of quality wine. In order to prevent the watering-down of Franconian wines during export, in 1726 the city council bottled vintage wine from the **Bürgerspital** in such bottles and stamped it with the city seal. Fraud was no longer an issue.

Local Wineries

The three largest Franconian wineries are located in Würzburg. All three enjoy a long, successful history and boast magnificent wine cellars and appellations. Moreover, they are part and parcel of the cultural sights in the city. At a glance:

Patrician families founded the **Bürgerspital** as a charitable institution in 1316 (pg. 73). In 1576 Julius Echter set up the **Juliusspital,** a second institution based on charity and winegrowing (pg. 68). The **Court Cellars** or **Hofkeller** in the Residence is reminiscent of the prince-bishops' penchant for wine (pg. 40).

All three offer **guided tours** of their historic cellars and each holds a **wine fest,** has **wine tastings** and **sells wine.**

Weingut am Stein Winery
Mittlerer Steinbergweg 5
Tel.: 0931 / 25808

www.weingut-am-stein.de

This family-owned winery is located at the foot of the Stein slopes. There

Left: A Wine Fest in the Bürgerspital courtyard.
Above: Picking premium grapes above the Old Town.

is a lovely view from the terrace over the entire city and wine fest events include funky music, blues, salsa and live bands.

> **TIP:** *Chef cook, Bernard Reiser, offers fine dining and exquisite cuisine at the Weinstein Wine Inn adjacent. Mittlerer Steinbergweg 5, Tel: 0931/286901.*

Further Winegrowers

A vinothek currently located on the bastion near the Old Crane offers an assortment of **Franconian wines** from local vintners, wineries and wine cooperatives from throughout the region.

Wine Inns and Pubs

Würzburg would not be the same without its traditional wine inns and pubs that attract young and old alike. In addition to the wine pubs at the three large wineries, there is the **Johanniterbäck** (Johanniterplatz 3, Tel: 0931/54368), **Weinstube Popp** (Textorstrasse 17, Tel: 0931/52425), **Sandertorbäck** (Sanderstrasse 18, Tel: 0931/13360), and **Weinhaus**

Schnabel (Haugerpfarrgasse 10, Tel: 0931/53314). The long tradition of bringing one's own sandwich continues at the **Maulaffenbäck** (Maulhardgasse 9, Tel: 0931/52351).

More Wine Fests and Events

Every spring a **wine village** is set up at the Market Place and the Cathedral holds a **wine parade.** The Franconian Vintners Association also sponsors a **Baroque Festival** in the Residence.

Stein-Wine Path

Beginning at the Mittlerer Steinbergweg near Weinhaus Knoll Winery, a **4-km wine path** with 25 info plaques guides the rambler through the Stein vineyards. There is a spectacular view from the top.

Beer

Although the emphasis has been on wine, the topic of beer should not be neglected. Literally every restaurant and café as well as wine inn serves this noble beverage. The two closest beer gardens are the **Würzburg-**

er Hofbräu Beer Garden in the Zellerau quarter (Jägerstrasse 17, Tel: 0931/42970) and the **beer garden** at the Old Crane.

Theater, Music, Dance and Cabaret

Mainfranken Theater
Theaterstrasse 21
Tel.: 0931 / 3908-0
www.theaterwuerzburg.de
The city theater features plays, ballet and musicals

Bockshorn in the Granary Museum
Veitshöchheimerstrasse 5
Tel: 0931 / 4606066
www.bockshorn.de
Cabaret, chansons, theater and music from budding stars to well-known performers

Kunstkeller Würzburg
Kroatengasse 20
Tel.: 0162 / 5634996
www.kunstkeller-wuerzburg.de
Out-of-the-ordinary theater, art gallery and music from well-known writers

Omnibus
Theaterstrasse 10
Tel.: 0931 / 56121
www.omnibus-wuerzburg.de
Live bands perform blues, soul, jazz and folk music in Würzburg's oldest music pub

tanzSpeicher Würzburg
Veltshöchhelmerstrasse 5
Tel.: 0931 / 4525855
www.tanzspeicherwuerzburg.de
The stage in the Granary Museum features experimental and modern dance

Theater am Neunerplatz
Adelgundenweg 2a
Tel.: 0931 / 4154 43
www.neunerplatz.de
Experimental, satirical and political theater for adults often with musical accompaniment

Left: Picking grapes on the fortress' south slope.
Above: Musical entertainment at the Hofgarten Wine Fest at the Residence.

Theater Chambinzky
Valentin-Becker-Strasse 2, Würzburg
Tel.: 0931 / 51212
www.chambinzky.com
Boulevard theater and folklore productions

theater ensemble
Frankfurterstrasse 87, Würzburg
Tel.: 0931 / 44545
www.theater-ensemble.net
Experimental and traditional plays and theater of the absurd as well as dramas and comedies

Werkstattbühne
Rüdigerstrasse 4, Würzburg
Tel.: 0931 / 59400
www.werkstattbuehne.com

The oldest of the small playhouses features classical and modern works with a critical flair

Children's Activites

Das Kasperhaus
Julius-Echter-Strasse 8, Würzburg
Tel.: 0931 / 3593494
www.theater-kasperhaus.de
Puppet theater for children

Punch and Judy Puppet Theater
Plastisches Theater Hobbit
Münzstrasse 1, Würzburg
Tel.: 0931 / 59830
www.theater-hobbit.de
Puppets, marionettes and masked performances for young and old

Farm Camp
Leistenstrasse, Würzburg
Tel.: 0931 / 76399
School days: Tues – Fri 14 – 18,
Sat 10 – 15
Vacation times: Mon – Fri 10 – 16
www.kinder-und-jugendfarm.de
Specializes in making handicrafts out of natural materials

Cultural Calendar
This calendar of events is by no means conclusive and does not contain the numerous open air productions

International Film Weekend
End of January in the downtown cinemas
Tel: 0931 / 15077
www.filmwochenende-wuerzburg.de
This festival is over 30 years old and features German and international films with subtitles

International Children's Fest
One day in May in the Old Town
Tel.: 0931 / 7948235
Fax: 09 31 / 7 94 81 60
www.dahw.de

Theater Spielberg
Reiserstrasse 7, Würzburg
Tel.: 09931 / 26645
www.theater-spielberg.de
Theater for children and teenagers; puppet shows for all ages

Theater am Neunerplatz
(see above info)
www.theater-spielberg.de
Children perform for children

Playgrounds
- Klein-Nizza in the Ring Park behind the Residence
- State Garden Show Gardens (entrance Zellerstrasse)
- Frankenwarte, Albert-Günther-Weg

Africa Festival
May/June at the Talavera Mainwiesen
Tel.: 0931 / 15060
www.africafestival.org
One of the highlights of the year: African and international music and culture featuring well-known artists and an international bazaar

Baroque Festival
Every May in the Residence
Tel.: 0931 / 3901111
www.frankenwein-aktuell.de
Franconian wines and culinary delights are served in the Residence

Above: A sandy beach in the heart of Würzburg at Lion's Bridge.

Würzburg Wine Village
In May/June at the Market Place
Tel.: 0931 / 72857
www.weindorf-wuerzburg.de
Over one hundred Franconian wines and culinary specialties are served in arbors at the Market Place

Mozart Festival
In May/June in the Residence and elsewhere
Tel.: 0931 / 372336
www.mozartfest-wuerzburg.de
This musical festival draws local as well as international music lovers. Tickets should be ordered well in advance. Bring a blanket to sit on at the two outdoor performances in the Residence gardens

Kiliani Fest
In July at the Talavera
Tel.: 0931 / 372695
www.Kiliani-Bierzelt.de
The largest carnival-like fair in Franconia in honor of St. Kilian; it opens with a parade of folk costumes through the downtown area

Italian Night
In July in the Residence
Tel.: 0931 / 3908124
www.theaterwuerzburg.de
Italian musical and culinary specialties

Würzburg Harbor Summer Festival
In August at the Old Harbor
Tel.: 0931 / 372781
www.wuerzburg.de
Open air cultural festival at the Old Harbor featuring music, theater and films

Ring Park Fest
In August at the Klein-Nizza
Tel.: 0931 / 372214; Fax: 09 31 / 37 35 89
www.wuerzburg.de
Live music of all kinds with special children's activities

Wine Parade
In August in the Old Town
Tel.: 0931 / 72857
www.weinparade.de
Local wineries serve their champagnes and wines along with hearty fare

Musical Street Festival
In September in the Old Town
Tel.: 0931 / 3534491
www.stramu-wuerzburg.de

Acrobatics, music and magic in the streets of the Old Town

City Fest
In September in the Old Town
Tel.: 0931/ 3536754
www.wuems.de
Stores present music, sport and games

Würzburg Night at the Residence
In October in the Residence
Tel.: 0931 / 355170
www.residenz-wuerzburg.de
Chamber music, guided tours and delicacies in the Residence

Würzburg Jazz Festival
In October in the Felix-Fechenbach House
Tel.: 0931 / 462 20
www.jazzini-wuerzburg.de
A week dedicated to jazz

Würzburg Bach Days
In November at Johannis Church
Tel.: 0931 / 322846
www.bachtage-wuerzburg.de
Superb music and performances

Würzburg Christmas Market
In December at the Market Place
Tel.: 0931 / 372693
www.wuerzburg.de
Christmas Market booths are set up in front of Mary's Chapel and the House to the Falcon. Artists and craftsmen set up their wares in front of the Town Hall

TIP: *Check out our website for current activities and events:*
www.wuerzburg.de/termine

Left: Lively music during the Africa Festival.
Middle: Folk costumes on parade during the Kiliani Festival in July.
Above: An outdoor Mozart concert in the Court Gardens of the Residence.

Tourist Information and Ticket Service

House to the Falcon, Market Place 9
Tel.: 0931 / 372398

Jan – Mar: Mon – Fri 10 – 16, Sat 10 – 14
Apr – Dec: Mon – Fri 10 – 18, Sat 10 – 14,
(Aug – Oct: Sat – 15)
May – Oct: Sun and holidays 10 – 14
www.wuerzburg.de/tourismus

Central Tourist Office

Congress Tourismus Wirtschaft
Am Congress Centrum, 97 070 Würzburg
Tel.: 0931 / 372335

Overnight Stays Hotel Reservations

Tel.: 0931 / 372371
www.wuerzburg.de/tourismus
or Tourist Information at the Market
Place

DJH Youth Hostel

Burkarderstrasse 44, 97082 Würzburg
Tel.: 0931 / 42590

Campingplatz Kalte Quelle

Winterhäuserstrasse 160
Tel.: 0931 / 65598

Campingplatz Kanu-Club

Mergentheimerstrasse 13b
Tel.: 0931 / 72536

Public Transportation

WVV-citypunkt in the Echter Gallery at
the corner of Juliuspromenade/
Dominikanerplatz
Mon – Fri 9 – 17
Sat 9 – 13:30
Bus/streetcar schedule:
Tel.: 0931 / 362320
www.wvv.de/verkehr/nahverkehr

Church Services and Mass

Kürschnerhof 2,
next to Neumünster Church
Tel.: 0931 / 38665700
Mon – Fri 10 – 18, Sat 10 – 14

Guided Old Town Strolls in English

Jan – Dec: Sat 13
May – Oct: Fri 13, Sat 13
Tickets & meeting point:
House to the Falcon at the Market Place

City Tours in German

regulary
Information: Tourist Information
and Ticket Service (see left)

Night Watchman Tours in German

Mid – Feb/Mar: Tue – Sat: 20
Apr – Dec: Tue – Sat 20 & 21;
meeting point:
Vierröhren Fountain/Town Hall
Tel.: 0931 / 409356
www.wuerzburger-nachtwaechter.de

Boat Excursions

Regular excursions to Veitshöchheim
in season. Docks at Kranenkai near
the Old Crane.
Other excursions available upon request.

Veitshöchheimer Personenschifffahrt
Tel.: 0931 / 55633

Schiffstouristik Würzburg
Tel.: 0931 / 58573

The complete text of this city guide was proofread by the publisher as well as the translator. Mistakes of whatever nature are not intentional and the publisher as well as the author/ translator cannot be held liable for any factual mistakes. We ask for your complete understanding in this matter.
Both the publisher and the author have done their utmost to ensure that this 8th edition is accurate and up to date. If you feel something is incorrect or needs updating, please feel free to contact us at eh@hahnstudios.de

Imprint: Eighth revised edition 2008   **ISBN 978-3-928645-61-4**

© **Elmar Hahn Verlag, Veitshöchheim – www.elmar-hahn-verlag.de**

All rights reserved. No part of this publication may be reproduced in any form or by any means, electronic, mechanical or otherwise.

Idea and concept: Klaus Schinagl, Veitshöchheim
Photography: Elmar Hahn, Veitshöchheim
                             except for: Nachlass Erich Heckel (page: 14);
                             Gerhard Launer WFL GmbH (page: 15);
                             Johannes Müller (page: 69); Thomas Dorn (page: 124 below)
Text: Christine Weisner, Würzburg
Layout/Litho: Design by Klaus Schinagl, Veitshöchheim
Printing and Production: Karo-Druck KG, Frangart, www.karo-druck.it